The Bible:
Its Authority
and Interpretation
in the Ecumenical Movement

The Bible

Its Authority
and Interpretation
in the Ecumenical Movement

edited by Ellen Flesseman-van Leer

Faith and Order Paper No. 99

World Council of Churches, Geneva

Cover design: Paul May

ISBN No. 2-8254-0643-0

Contents

Preface

What place is to be assigned to the Bible in the life of the Church? What is its authority and in what way is it to be interpreted today? These questions have had a central place in the ecumenical movement from the beginning. Again and again they were debated at ecumenical consultations and conferences. During the last two decades in particular they have been the subject of intensive reflection within the Faith and Order Commission of the World Council of Churches. A series of studies was undertaken which led to significant clarifications and convergences. As reports of these studies have been published in various places and are perhaps not easily accessible, the Faith and Order Commission decided to bring them together, and this volume is the result.

In the first place, the Bible is a uniting factor. Every church engaged in the ecumenical movement appeals to the Bible as the authoritative basis of its faith, life and witness. Each regards it as the unique source of knowledge about the revelation in Jesus Christ. As they seek to overcome their differences, therefore, the churches can turn together to the Bible. In the light of the biblical witness they can re-examine their positions and re-think together the controversies which have caused separation in the past and continue to keep them divided today. As they re-read the Bible together they will discover dimensions and aspects whose neglect has led to one-sided emphases, and they will help one another to arrive at a fuller understanding of the truth. The explicit reference to the Bible which was added to the Basis of the World Council of Churches in 1961 is, therefore, more than a formality. It is the expression of a deep reality. It points, on the one hand, to the fact that, across the boundaries of traditions, the churches are held together by their common allegiance to the Bible; and, on the other hand, it points to the hope that, in that fellowship of common allegiance, they will find ways of advancing together towards fuller unity.

As they turn together to the Bible, the churches will inevitably be confronted with the issue of the authority and the right interpretation of the Bible. Two considerations are of particular importance in this respect.

1. The churches differ in their approach to the Bible. Though they all recognize its authority, they hold different views on the way it is to be understood. In particular, they assess differently the respective authority and interaction of criteria like the Bible, the creeds and confessional statements, the magisterium and the common mind of the Church. Consequently, though reading the same Bible, the churches can easily arrive at different conclusions. Ultimately, therefore, they can overcome their differences and restore communion only if they succeed in defining together the appropriate approach to the Bible. This is particularly obvious for the encounter between the Roman Catholic Church and the churches of the Reformation; but it is also true for the encounter between other churches. To reach deeper mutual understanding, the churches need to develop a common mind on the role which the Bible is to play in the life of the Church.

2. The issue is pressed upon the churches for another reason. How can they, on the basis of the Bible, bear witness today? In particular, how can they give a common testimony on social and political issues arising in the contemporary world? As they engage in the search for communion, the churches cannot postpone their common witness until the day when that communion will be restored. They must already now form a fellowship of witness and begin to respond together to the challenges of their time. As they seek to speak and act together they will be confronted again with their different approaches to the Bible; the response to contemporary issues will raise ever new problems which further complicate the common task. They many be able to state together certain convictions which they hold in common but they will not easily be able to show convincingly how their pronouncements have been derived from the Bible. It is not surprising, therefore, that ecumenical statements are sometimes criticized for an alleged lack of biblical foundation. In fact, the reason for this apparent weakness lies with the churches and their divergent approaches to the Bible. To form a fellowship of effective common witness it is essential that the churches reach a common understanding of the mayhority and the use of the Bible in the life and witness of the Church.

The reports gathered in this volume reflect a nascent "tradition" of common reflection. Over a period of many years Christians from different churches have sought to develop common perspectives on the authority of the Bible. Considerable progress has been achieved. It has become clear that many of the old controversies regarding the scriptures are not as definitive as had been thought. But obviously, the convergences which can be discerned in these reports are still not more than a beginning. It has often been said that for the restoration of unity the churches need to develop "common ways of teaching and decision-making". The common reflection on the Bible is a contribution towards meeting this requirement. It is an indispensable ingredient if the question is to be answered in what way the Church today can know and communicate the truth revealed in Jesus Christ. But the reflection needs to be pursued; in order for the requirement to be fulfilled, it will need to be accompanied and strengthened by a fresh examination of the authority of creeds and confessions, of the role of the ministry and the Church as a whole.

The present volume has been prepared by Dr Ellen Flesseman-van Leer. She has also written the introduction which surveys the whole material. Having participated in all stages of the reflection, she is particularly qualified to present the reports to the reader. I wish to express to her the gratitude of the Faith and Order Commission for undertaking this task. At the same time I wish to thank all those who, by their collaboration in the course of the years, have contributed to building this "tradition of common ecumenical reflection".

31 December 1979   LUKAS VISCHER

Introduction

Biblical theology

During the Second World War, the churches, especially the Reformation churches in Europe, had, as it were, rediscovered the relevance of the Bible. It had given them support and guidance in the midst of the perplexities and dangers of that dark time. They brought this experience into the thinking of the newly-founded World Council of Churches, and so in its early years much serious study was devoted to the Bible. People like Hendrik Kraemer and Suzanne de Dietrich played an important role in promoting this approach to the Bible. The impact of their work was not restricted to the Ecumenical Institute at Bossey and the World Council but went far beyond their confines. The common conviction underlying this biblical movement was that the Bible spoke to all issues, if only people were willing to listen carefully to what it had to say.

It was in this climate that the Study Department of the World Council of Churches organized several conferences to study such questions as the nature of biblical authority for various realms of modern life, the correct interpretation of the Bible, the relation between the Old and the New Testaments. The outcome was a report entitled *Guiding Principles for the Interpretation of the Bible*, produced at Wadham College, Oxford, in 1949. This report represents a good example of the emphasis on "biblical theology" which was generally accepted in World Council circles for more than a decade and a half. The approach combined a historical interpretation of the biblical texts with a confessing theology, and stressed the unity of the two Testaments as the faithful and uncorrupted witness to God's history of salvation. Its chief characteristic was its christocentric emphasis: Jesus Christ is seen as the key to the interpretation of the Bible, since He is its centre and its goal.

The report spells out the essential theological assumptions for our approach to the Bible if we are to understand it aright. First and foremost is the conviction that in the Bible we are confronted with the living Word of God. On this assumption, of course, no further argument is required to show that the Bible has authority. Although the report warns against the temptation of appealing in too facile a manner to biblical texts and of harmonizing too readily their divergent witnesses, it does not hesitate to speak of *the* biblical message or doctrine.

The report is optimistic in tone. Of course, it clearly recognizes the distance between the context in which the Bible spoke and the problems confronting us today, but it is confident that the Bible can guide us to the knowledge of God's will in every situation.

Tradition and Scripture

When this confidence in the Bible's unifying power was put to the test, however, the problems turned out to be more intractable than the biblical movement in its elan and optimism had foreseen. It became clear that agreement on the context of the biblical message and especially on the ways of applying it to contemporary issues was not within easy reach. The confessional traditions, all claiming biblical support for their positions, continued to determine the reading of the Bible. The biblical texts can never be interpreted *ab ovo*; interpretation is always conditioned by the tradition within which the interpreter stands. This insight provided the impetus for a new approach to the problem: a study of the relation between Tradition and Scripture was launched.

The confessional traditions are divided in their understanding of the relation between Tradition and Scripture. Where is revealed truth to be found? Are there two sources of knowledge — Tradition and Scripture? Or only one single source — Scripture? The issue, for centuries a point of controversy, acquired new relevance in those years. It was one of the important issues taken up for debate by the Second Vatican Council.

The report of the Fourth World Conference on Faith and Order in Montreal (1963), *Scripture, Tradition and Traditions*, succeeded in formulating new common perspectives. It proved helpful to differentiate between Tradition (with a capital "T"), meaning the Gospel itself transmitted from generation to generation in and by the Church, and traditions (with a small "t"), meaning the churches' diverse expressions of the one Tradition. This distinction made possible a more dynamic view of Tradition and its relation to Scripture. Tradition was accordingly understood not as a sum of tenets fixed once and for all and transmitted from generation to generation, but rather as a living reality, God's revelation in Christ and its course through history. In other words, God's revelation in the past is accessible today only as Tradition. To quote the best-known words of the report: "We exist as Christians by the Tradition of the Gospel (the *paradosis* of the *kerygma*)" (p. 21

paragraph 45). But we do not possess this Tradition in and by itself; it comes to us in the form of our confessional traditions. The question arises, therefore, as to whether and to what extent the various traditions are embodiments of the Tradition, i.e. whether and to what extent they faithfully transmit revelation. The report here points to the scriptures. The Bible is, as it were, Tradition written down at an early stage in its course through the ages. In the words of the report: "The criterion for the genuine Tradition (is to be found) in the holy scriptures rightly interpreted" (p.23 paragraph 51). This at once raises the question, what is right interpretation? The opinions of the churches on this question vary considerably, as the enumeration of the different hermeneutical principles in the report clearly shows.

The significance of the report lies in the recognition that Tradition and Scripture are not two independent entities. They are so intertwined that neither one of them, taken in itself, can simply be used as authoritative. The Reformation principle of *sola scriptura* is qualified by the reminder that the Bible is part of Tradition and embedded in Tradition; in fact it becomes living Tradition as it is rightly interpreted in ever new situations. On the other hand, Tradition as source of revelation is qualified by the assertion that it is only accessible in traditions whose trustworthiness must be tested in the light of Scripture. One of the most far-reaching differences between the "protestant" and "catholic" views is being bridged by this double qualification. The weight of this rapprochement is all the greater since the Faith and Order Conference at Montreal was the first one in which the Orthodox churches fully participated and the Roman Catholic tradition began to be represented.

The report received wide recognition and had a certain influence on the formulation of the Dogmatic Constitution on Divine Revelation of Vatican II. Since then the old controversy on Tradition has subsided.

The report generated two lines of further study: it led, on the one hand, to a study of the Fathers and their importance for theology, a study which was followed up later by a close examination of the Council of Chalcedon, and, on the other hand, it led to the various reports on the interpretation and authority of the Bible which are reproduced in this booklet.

The fresh study of the authority and appropriate use of the Bible was not only due to the breakthrough on the issue of Tradition and Scripture but was also prompted by a debate in one of the plenary sessions on "ecclesiology in the New Testament". Two speakers, Ernst Käsemann and Raymond E. Brown, addressed the conference on the subject and the debate which followed underlined the urgent need for a study of biblical interpretation. Using the tools of modern historical and literary criticism, both scholars, the one a Lutheran, the other a Roman Catholic, pointed out the diversity of ecclesiologies in the New Testament. While agreed on this point, they differed in that Brown still stressed the common elements in this diversity, whereas Käsemann made a conscious and admitted choice on the basis of his prior theological understanding of the Church. His position met with considerable opposition at the conference; some even feared that, if his position was accepted generally, it would spell the end of all attempts to achieve the unity of the Church. His position met with considerable opposition at the conference; some even feared that, if his position was accepted generally, it would spell the end of all attempts to achieve the unity of the Church.

Thus, Montreal not only offered a new approach to the old problem of Scripture and Tradition, but also broke fresh ground in respect of the Bible. Three connected insights are of special importance in this regard:

1. The role played by confessional traditions in determining the interpretation of the Bible was more clearly recognized. Attention was drawn to the different hermeneutical keys used by various churches; in fact the Montreal report even specified some of them.

2. It seems impossible to speak univocally any more of *the* biblical message or *the* biblical doctrine in respect of a particular issue.

3. The importance of critical biblical scholarship was affirmed and the insight that the use of this exegetical tool had far-reaching *theological* consequences was brought home.

These relatively new insights set the question of the interpretation and place of the Bible in a new perspective.

The Montreal conference also lodged another issue firmly on the agenda of the World Council of Churches. It dealt extensively with the reinterpretation of the Christian faith in different cultures; the whole of the third part of the report is devoted to that subject. Tradition, the first part of the report had argued, is the constant reinterpretation of the message handed down by the apostles; "a mere reiteration of the words of Holy Scripture would be a betrayal of the Gospel" (p. 23 paragraph 50). The task of indigenizing the Gospel already recognized earlier was thus provided with a firmer theological basis and fresh impulses. In the succeeding years, as the participation of the younger churches in the theological debate became more effective and the encounter of cultures became more central, the issue was to be further developed.

Hermeneutics

The interpretative rules of biblical exegesis laid down in the Wadham report no longer appeared adequate, for the reasons indicated above. It became imperative to take up once again the question of right interpretation. Therefore, an extensive study programme on hermeneutics was initiated immediately after the Montreal conference. High hopes were placed on this programme; common hermeneutical rules would, it was hoped, lead to a common approach to the Bible and in this way advance the cause of Christian unity. The fruits of this study were summarized in the report "The Significance of the Hermeneutical Problem for the Ecumenical Movement", which was presented to the Bristol Faith and Order Commission meeting in 1967. As was to be expected after Montreal, the report wholeheartedly acknowledges the generally accepted process of scholarly exegesis which makes use of literary and historical criticism and draws the theological consequences from that criticism. The change in theological climate after Montreal can be gauged by comparing the Wadham report with the Bristol report. The major part of the earlier report dealt with the necessary theological presuppositions of biblical interpretation, whereas the Bristol report makes no reference whatever to theological presuppositions; the exegetical process which it describes is in the main valid equally for both biblical and other literary documents. In the first and most specific section, dealing with hermeneutics, the consensus presented is dominated by the acknowledgment that the Bible is a collection of *human* writings.

As was also to be expected from a study ensuing from the Montreal conference, special attention is given to the issue of unity and diversity. This, too, is an aspect which heralds a new development. To be sure, the Wadham report had also recognized a certain degree of diversity in the Bible, but this diversity was not considered to be a theologically relevant or even perhaps a positive factor, but rather something to be surmounted in order to discern the common biblical testimony. In the Bristol report this diversity is given full weight. There are diverse literary traditions in the biblical writings. They may be complementary, each one illuminating particular aspects of the truth; in this case they are a true enrichment of our understanding of its many-sidedness. But the report does not preclude the possibility that some of these traditions may be contradictory, in which case we have to decide for or against a particular concept. This recognition of diversity, which precludes any facile harmonization of texts, was to have far-reaching consequences in ecclesiological thinking in the following years. A first indication of this is already to be found in the Bristol report when it notes that one contributory factor to the confessional divisions of the churches may well be the differences already present within the biblical canon.

Biblical authority

All churches attribute authority to the Bible. It was on this authority that the Wadham document based its interpretative principles. Since then, new insights had been gained which made it necessary to reflect more deeply on the concept. It could no longer simply be taken for granted. In part this was due to what may be called the general crisis of authority in those years. But a more immediate and weighty reason was provided by the unresolved questions raised by the study on hermeneutics. We mention three such issues:

1. When pointing to the diversity of traditions within the Bible, the Bristol report had not ruled out the possibility that we may be compelled to decide for or against a particular concept. Obviously, this has implications for the traditional view of biblical authority.

2. The Bristol report had focused attention on the methodology of exegesis. It had come to the conclusion that biblical scholars, when approaching a text, apply more or less the same rules. But differences begin to appear when they try to apply the texts to the contemporary life of the churches. In other words, the real problems only arise after the basic exegetical work has been completed. The report points out that these differences have their roots in the varying importance given to the biblical text as a document of faith.

3. Finally, critical scholarship had made people aware of the historical gulf separating them today from the biblical writings. In the course of the study on hermeneutics the question had been raised but no satisfactory answer given as to how this gulf can be bridged and, more radically still, whether it is possible, or even necessary, to bridge it at all. The answer we give to these questions depends once again on our view of biblical authority.

In the light of these considerations, it came as no surprise that the meeting of the Faith and Order Commission at Bristol (1967), which accepted the report on hermeneutics, recommended that it be followed up by a study on the authority of the Bible.

The recommendation was acted upon and several study groups were established whose work eventually led to the report on "The Authority of the Bible" submitted to the Faith and Order Commission at its following meeting in Louvain (1971).

The most important feature of this report is its emphasis on the character of authority. The following three points show this most clearly:

1. In its most specific sense, when the Bible is seen not as aliterary or historical document but as a force capable of leading people to faith, the authority of the Bible is not a fixed quality belonging to the Bible *per se*. It must be understood as a "relational concept". In other words, authority is a present reality only when it is experienced as authority, though at the same time it transcends human experience (p. 49). Evidently, the report does not

equate this authority with a human value judgment on the Bible. It is rather that the impact of the biblical testimony itself demonstrates its authority, which is ultimately the authority of God.

2. When biblical authority is discussed, inevitably the question of the significance of the canon needs to be taken up, since it is to particular canonical writings that authority is ascribed. Earlier reports had avoided this issue. The report "The Authority of the Bible" is the first to pay explicit attention to it. Also in this respect the report emphasizes the dynamic character of authority. While fully recognizing the importance of the canon for the life of the Church, the report at the same time insists that the dividing line between canonical and non-canonical writings is not a hard and fast one. The fact that the churches do not all have exactly the same canon is therefore only of relative importance. In any case, it is not a legitimate ground for the churches to remain divided.

3. The dynamic character of authority is further demonstrated by the way in which the report deals with the inspiration of scriptures. None of the previous reports had even mentioned inspiration though the Wadham and Montreal reports had certainly tacitly assumed Scripture was inspired. The report on the authority of the Bible breaks new ground in this regard, devoting a whole section to the subject. Traditionally, the basis of the authority of the Bible had been seen in the fact of its inspiration. Inspiration had been treated as an *a priori* dogmatic presupposition. Now inspiration is affirmed not as a starting point or as an argument on which biblical authority can be based, but as a conclusion of faith. Because, in the Bible, God's claim is being experienced in a compelling way, the conclusion can be drawn that his own activity, that is, the activity of his Spirit, must be behind it. In other words: the assertion of inspiration is based on the experience that the Bible and its message have proved themselves authoritative. Here again, an earlier more static way of thinking has been left behind.

The Louvain report also takes up and develops a number of points mentioned in the report on hermeneutics. The differences and possible contradictions between biblical texts, for example, to which the earlier report had referred, are now qualified and put into clearer perspective by the insight that the biblical traditions, in all their variety, all point beyond themselves to God. The report also offers a criterion for judging the value of differing texts: namely, the degree to which a particular text interprets a central saving event attested in the scriptures. The acceptance of the view that critical distinction can be made within the biblical material is in accord with the dynamic character of authority to which we have drawn attention.

Ever since Montreal the question had been discussed whether there is a specific centre of Holy Scripture providing the key for the interpretation of the whole. The Louvain report suggests that there is not just one such centre, but that different sets of statements and different biblical writings each have different decisive centres. In more technical terminology: whereas the concepts of "canon within the canon" or "material centre" (*Sachmitte*) are rejected, the idea of a number of relational centres (*Beziehungsmitten*) is put forward (p. 52 III, 7).

As we have seen, the Bristol report remained vague when it came to describing how the biblical text can be brought to life in the teaching and preaching of the Church. The Louvain report provides further clarification here too, not by establishing specific guidelines but by suggesting that we today should enter into the process of interpretation in which the biblical witnesses themselves were engaged. In this connection the report employs the idea of the "prolongation of the interpretative process". At first glance, the expression is open to misunderstanding. Does it not impair the unique place of the Bible? The report, however, contains enough safeguards against this misinterpretation. In fact, the idea of an ongoing process of interpretation is nothing else than a concrete way of articulating the broad notion of Tradition as defined by the Montreal conference.

Finally, the report underlines the importance of the situation for the interpretation of the Bible. The role of the context had already been recognized in earlier reports. The recognition was presupposed for instance when the Montreal conference discussed the issue of indigenization. The Louvain report goes a step further; the insight that the contemporary situation and its particular problems are an indispensable hermeneutical category is not only recognized in general terms but developed in concise formulations.

The Old Testament

The question of the importance of the Old Testament has always figured in ecumenical discussions, for the simple reason that the churches differ in their approach to the Old Testament and that these differences lie at the root of other differences which divide them in the theological as well as the social and political realms. Two important examples may be mentioned:

1. For many years, the relationship between the Church and the Jewish people has been a subject of hot debate both within and between the churches. A wide range of positions divides the churches. Obviously, the possibility of mutual understanding would be considerably enhanced if agreement could be achieved as to the way the Old Testament is to be appealed to in this debate.

2. Again and again, representatives of non-western churches have drawn attention to the fact that the Old Testament did not play the same role in the life of their churches as in the churches of the West. Specifically, the need for indigenizing the Christian message raised the question of the specific value to be attributed to the Old Testament by comparison to the religious writings and traditions of the indigenous cultures.

But despite the importance and relevance of these issues, of all the earlier reports on the Bible, only the Wadham report showed real interest in the Old Testament. Certainly the Montreal and Bristol reports referred in their considerations to both Old and New Testaments but they remained silent on the inter-relation between the two Testaments and one has the impression that the apostolic writings were their primary concern. The report on the authority of the Bible went a step further; it pointed to the different assessments of the Old Testament in the churches and noted that this resulted in important differences of interpretation. Prompted by this consideration, the Louvain meeting strongly recommended an ecumenical study on the Old Testament.

The last report included in this volume, "The Significance of the Old Testament in its Relation to the New", is the result of this study; it was produced at Loccum in 1977 and accepted by the Faith and Order Standing Commission at its meeting in Bangalore the following year.

The quintessence of the report is its insistence that the Old Testament is an integral and indispensable part of the one authoritative Scripture and that even after the coming of Christ it has become neither obsolete nor antiquated nor should it be regarded merely as a preparation for Christ. This affirmation is undergirded in the report by a reference to what it calls the "specificity" of the Old Testament, meaning those elements of the Old Testament in which it surpasses the New. By maintaining in this way the inherent importance of the Old Testament in and by itself, the report clearly goes beyond the Wadham guidelines. For these guidelines, by regarding Christology as the exclusive hermeneutical key, restricted so to say the significance of the Old Testament. The Loccum report, on the contrary, regards Christology as one among several central themes. It also leads to a deeper appreciation of the place of the Old Testament by showing that the notion of fulfilment is much more complex and differentiated than was formerly realized.

The report builds on the previous studies on hermeneutics and biblical authority; in part it adopts previous views, in part it develops them further. In the Bristol report the importance of the historical-critical method was assumed and many of its exegetical implications were worked out. In the Louvain report we already find an awareness that historical criticism is not the only possible scholarly approach to the Bible. In the Loccum report reference is made to yet other hermeneutical approaches which have come to the fore in recent years, such as the literary approach, or the political approach employed especially by Latin American theologians. A new feature is the reference to the use of Scripture in the liturgy of the churches and in the devotional life of Christians; it counteracts a too one-sided intellectual approach to the Bible. Attention is also given to the attitude of almost unquestioning contemporaneity with which many African Christians read the Bible.

This recognition of the variety of hermeneutical approaches is probably a feature of the report which in its full import will become manifest only in the future. For it may well be that in continuing the ecumenical reflection on the Bible, primary attention will have to be given to the ways in which the Bible is used and interpreted by Christians in different cultures. Already in this report, in fact, more attention is paid to the non-western churches than in earlier documents.

Reference was made in the Louvain report to the interpretative process which began in the Bible and was continued in the transmission of the biblical message in the churches. The Loccum report substantiates this thought by dealing with the re-reading of Old Testament texts in the New Testament. And, by pointing out that the New Testament writers used various exegetical methods which were current in their day but are not acceptable now, the report implicitly suggests that modern methods of interpretation may also have their appointed time. This is in fact borne out by the changes which have occurred since the Wadham conference.

A final point worth mentioning here is that the report seems to reflect a renewed interest in the theological unity of the Bible. After the Second World War, a unified view of the Bible was the commonly accepted premise. At the Montreal World Conference on Faith and Order in 1963, it became clear that, in the view of biblical scholarship, this unity was based on too facile a harmonization of texts. In the subsequent years, prominence was given to the diversity of the biblical material. The Loccum report now reminds us that this diversity is not the last word. The unity of biblical truth, reflected in the very plurality of the biblical witnesses, must be remembered.

The relevance of the reports

At the conclusion of this survey, it may be helpful to reflect on the relevance of the thoughts developed in these reports and the impact they had. Their potential importance for the thinking of the churches can be great indeed, but it cannot yet be gauged. Ecumenical insights are taken up only gradually by the churches. Their impact, therefore, will have to be discovered in the future by the extent to which the clues given in the reports are developed and become fruitful in various local situations.

But even within the World Council of Churches the thoughts of these reports are not yet assimilated. They could influence the whole understanding of the ecumenical movement, in its mission, its educational programmes, the debate on the relation of faith and culture, the way in which Bible study is done. The one thing, however, which is already possible is to give some examples of their impact on the thinking of the Faith and Order Commission.

1. The reports have given rise to a change in the use of the Bible. The conviction that everything said together must be grounded in the Bible remains unimpaired. But being grounded in the Bible is today understood as being in accord with the overall thinking and climate of the Bible, that is, arising out of the message of the Bible as a whole. Therefore, today, greater store is set on Faith and Order documents being imbued with a biblical spirit than giving many textual quotations. The hermeneutical studies have helped us to realize that the diversity of traditions in the Bible makes it difficult to work with proof texts. They have taught us, moreover, that a careful analysis of the literary and contextual background of each text is required before it can be quoted and that no text is directly applicable to any present-day dogmatic or ethical question. It can be said that, as a consequence, the Faith and Order Commission has become more restrained but also more responsible in quoting the Bible, so that fewer explicit textual quotations will be found in recent documents.

2. In the Bristol report mention was already made of the bearing which the recognition of diversity in the Bible might have on a deeper understanding of Church unity. The concept of conciliar fellowship, which was developed in later years, proved the truth of this insight. This concept has been employed as a description of the ultimate goal of unity. It commended itself because it recognizes the diversity of the churches which, reinterpreting one and the same truth, each in its own culture and situation, are mutually accountable and called to correct, encourage and complement each other in permanent consultation. The correspondence with the emphasis on biblical diversity in the reports is obvious; within the one canon different traditions are found, each testifying to the same Gospel but no single one in itself representing its full richness. Yet this diversity within the Bible does not detract from the underlying unity of the Bible, as the Loccum report points out. The ecclesiological counterpart to this renewed emphasis on biblical unity is the insistence that the unity of the churches must find visible expression.

3. The emphasis of the Louvain report on the role of the context in the process of interpretation has had a considerable impact on the work of the Faith and Order Commission. It has made possible a constructive biblical approach to the contextual theologies which have emerged in the past two decades, for example, black theology, liberation theology, feminist theology. More particularly, it has played a significant role in shaping the Faith and Order study "Giving Account of the Hope". This project was initiated in 1972 when the Faith and Order Commission addressed an invitation to churches, church groups and individual Christians all over the world to indicate the way in which they articulated their hope in Christ in their specific situations. By starting from specific situation-bound testimonies, the study sought to do justice both to the basic unity and to the contextuality of the Christian message. In this way the insights of the Louvain report on the authority of the Bible were made operative in an actual study process. Many responses to the invitation were received in the following years and on the basis of these specific accounts the Commission produced, at its Bangalore meeting in 1978, a "Common Account of Hope". This text is an attempt to give expression to the *one* hope in the multiplicity of its concrete expressions; it is at the same time contextual, as it addresses itself to the common situation of the contemporary world in which the churches live. In fact, the common account can be fully appreciated only if it is read together with the specific testimonies.

4. The "Common Account of Hope" concludes for the time being the study "Giving Account of the Hope". The whole process quite naturally leads to another issue. How does the Church give expression to "one apostolic faith" which is the basis of its unity and its witness? As it pursues the goal of visible unity it is imperative that the Faith and Order Commission turn its attention to this task. A host of questions will immediately arise. How does the one Church, in theory and practice, recognize the Bible as the authority under which it lives? How does it confess the one apostolic faith today? What authority does it attribute to the ecumenical creeds? Are they sufficient as confession of faith or do they need to be supplemented or even replaced by contemporary, more fully elaborated, confessions of faith? Is there need for *one* confession of faith providing the basis of the unity of the Church or can the unity in the apostolic faith be safeguarded by a multiplicity of confessions? To answer these questions, the insights gained in the series of studies on the authority and the interpretation of the scriptures will be of crucial importance. No answer will be valid which does not take them sufficiently into account.

1. Guiding Principles for the Interpretation of the Bible

Accepted by the Ecumenical Study Conference, held at Wadham College, Oxford, from 29 June to 5 July 1949.

In the years following the Second World War, the Study Department of the World Council of Churches organized several ecumenical study conferences on the ethical and political message of the Bible for the modern world: London in 1946, Bossey in 1947, Zetten (Netherlands) in 1948 and Wadham College, Oxford, in 1949. Most major church traditions were represented at these meetings, with the notable exception of the Roman Catholic Church. The document reproduced here represents the consensus reached in the course of the four consultations. It was first published in *The Ecumenical Review*, Vol. II, 1950, No. 1, pp. 81-86. The report of the first two meetings can be found in the pamphlet, *From the Bible to the Modern World* (published by the WCC Study Department, Geneva, 1947).

*   *
*

Our conference has endeavoured, on the basis of the work of earlier conferences, to develop specific principles of interpretation, for the use of the Bible in relation to social and political questions. The Christian's authority lies in the will of God. It is agreed that the Bible stands in a unique position in mediating that will to us. In our study together we have used Jer. 7:1-15 as a test case in discovering the extent of agreement in the application of hermeneutical principles. We have found a measure of agreement that surprised us all. We submit the following statements as a general consensus.

I. The necessary theological presuppositions of biblical interpretation

a) It is agreed that the Bible is our common starting point, for there God's Word confronts us, a Word which humbles the hearers so that they are more ready to listen and to discuss than they are to assert their own opinions.

b) It is agreed that the primary message of the Bible concerns God's gracious and redemptive activity for the saving of sinful man that He might create in Jesus Christ a people for himself. In this, the Bible's central concern, an authoritative claim is placed upon man and he is called upon to respond in faith and obedience throughout the whole of his life and work. The law of love has always a binding and compelling hold upon us, and in it we encounter the inescapable will of God. On the other hand, in the more specific laws provided for the detailed organization of the social life of a people who lived under conditions different from our own, we should through reverent and serious study seek to distinguish in the light of God's revelation in Christ the permanently binding from that of purely local and temporal significance.

c) It is agreed that the starting point of the Christian interpreter lies within the redeemed community of which by faith he is a member.

d) It is agreed that the centre and goal of the whole Bible is Jesus Christ. This gives the two Testaments a perspective in which Jesus Christ is seen both as the fulfilment and the end of the Law.

e) It is agreed that the unity of the Old and the New Testaments is not to be found in any naturalistic development, or in any static identity, but in the ongoing redemptive activity of God in the history of one people, reaching its fulfilment in Christ. Accordingly it is of decisive importance for hermeneutical method to interpret the Old Testament in the light of the total revelation in the person of Jesus Christ, the Incarnate Word of God, from which arises the full trinitarian faith of the Church.

f) It is agreed that allegorical interpretations which were not intended by the biblical authors are arbitrary and their use may be a disservice to the proper recognition of biblical authority. But Christian exegesis has been justified in recognizing as divinely established a certain correspondence between some events and teachings of the Old and of the New Testament.

g) It is agreed that, although we may differ in the manner in which tradition, reason and natural law may be used in the interpretation of Scripture, any teaching that clearly contradicts the biblical position cannot be accepted as Christian.

II. The interpretation of a specific passage

a) It is agreed that one must start with an historical and critical examination of the passage. This includes:

1) the determination of the text;
2) the literary form of the passage;
3) the historical situation, the *Sitz im Leben;*

4) the meaning which the words had for the original author and hearer or reader;

5) the understanding of the passage in the light of its total context and the background out of which it emerged.

b) It is agreed that in the case of an Old Testament passage, one must examine and expound it in relation to the revelation of God to Israel both before and after its own period. Then the interpreter should turn to the New Testament in order to view the passage in that perspective. In this procedure the Old Testament passage may receive limitation and correction, and it may also disclose in the light of the New Testament a new and more profound significance, unknown to the original writer.

c) It is agreed that in the case of a New Testament passage one should examine it in the light of its setting and context; then turn to the Old Testament to discover its background in God's former revelation. Returning again to the New Testament one is able to see and expound the passage in the light of the whole scope of *Heilsgeschichte*. Here our understanding of a New Testament passage may be deepened through our apprehension of the Old.

III. The discovery of the biblical teaching on a specific social or political issue

a) It is agreed that one must begin with a direct study of the biblical text in relation to a given problem; otherwise the general principles which we establish will reflect more the presuppositions of our own time than the message of the Bible. Only then may we safely deduce applications for our own situation.

b) It is agreed that in examining a particular modern problem we should begin with the New Testament teaching. In the light of this we should consider the Old Testament evidence as well, in order to view the problem in the light of God's total revelation. In following this procedure, historical differences in the various parts of Scripture must not be overlooked; otherwise the amassing of various texts may be done in too facile a manner and the Bible made to present a united witness on a topic which in fact it does not do. Furthermore, care should be used to see the correct proportions so that too much emphasis may not be placed on a single passage and the correct biblical perspective be lost.

c) It is agreed that the biblical teaching on social and political issues must be viewed in the light of the tension between life in the kingdoms of this world and participation in the Kingdom of God. While there has not been time in this conference to explore our understanding of the relation of ethics to eschatology, we are agreed that the scriptural teaching of the two ages has an important bearing upon the way in which a specific social or political issue is to be interpreted.

IV. The application of the biblical message to the modern world

a) It is agreed that if we are to receive the guidance of the Holy Spirit through the scriptures, we must discover the degree to which our particular situation is similar to that which the Bible presents. It must be remembered that absolute identity of situation is never found, and therefore the problem of adaptation becomes acute. Nevertheless in each new situation we must allow ourselves to be guided by the Bible to a knowledge of the will of God.

b) It is agreed that the Bible speaks primarily to the Church, but it also speaks through the Church to the world inasmuch as the whole world is claimed by the Church's Lord. The Church can best speak to the world by becoming the Church remade by the Word of God.

c) It is agreed that in applying the biblical message to our day, interpreters diverge because of differing doctrinal and ecclesiastical traditions, differing ethical, political, and cultural outlooks, differing geographical and sociological situations, differing temperaments and gifts. It is, however, an actual experience within the ecumenical movement, that when we meet together, with presuppositions of which we may be largely unconscious, and bring these presuppositions to the judgment of Scripture, some of the very difficulties are removed which prevent the Gospel from being heard. Thus the Bible itself leads us back to the living Word of God.

MEMBERS OF THE CONFERENCE

Prof. C.T. Craig, Madison, NJ, USA
Prof. V.E. Devadutt, Serampore, Bengal, India
Prof. C.H. Dodd, Cambridge, England
Prof. W. Eichrodt, Basle, Switzerland
Prof. G. Florovsky, New York, USA
Prof. J. Marsh, Oxford, England
Dr G. Mayeda, Japan
D. L. Munby, Oxford, England
Prof. N.W. Porteous, Edinburgh, Scotland
Canon A. Richardson, Durham, England (*Chairman*)
Prof. E. Schlink, Heidelberg, Germany
Dr W. Schweitzer, Geneva, Switzerland (*Secretary*)
Rev. O.S. Tomkins, London, England
Dr T.F. Torrance, Aberdeen, Scotland

Prof. L.J. Trinterud, Chicago, USA
Prof. G.E. Wright, Chicago, USA

PRESENT ONLY ON THE LAST DAYS
Bishop A. Nygren, Lund, Sweden
Prof. G. Staehlin, Erlangen, Germany

YOUTH DELEGATES
A. Adegbola, Nigeria
J.A. Atger, Saint-Martin-le-Vinoux par Grenoble, France
N.S. Booth, Boston, USA
J. Gibbs, Preston, England

2. Scripture, Tradition and Traditions

In accordance with the proposal of the Third World Conference on Faith and Order in Lund (1952) "to explore more deeply the resources to be found in that common history which we have as Christians and which we have discovered to be longer, larger and richer than any of our separate histories", a Theological Commission on "Tradition and Traditions" was set up. It worked over the following years through two study groups, one in Europe and the other in North America, under the chairmanship respectively of K.E. Skydsgaard and A.C. Outler. In 1961 the Commission published an interim report, *The Old and the New in the Church* (Faith and Order Paper No. 34, SCM Press, London) and in 1963 its final report, *Tradition and Traditions* (Faith and Order Paper No. 40). Both reports were submitted to Section II of the Fourth World Conference on Faith and Order in Montreal, 1963. Additional background material for this section was a document entitled "Extracts from Regional Studies" (mimeographed copy in the WCC Library Archives, Montreal, July 1963, Section II/3), dealing particularly with problems of indigenization. To guide the discussion at the conference, a special working paper (*ibid.* Section II/1) had been prepared. The conference drafted and accepted the report which is reproduced here; it was first published in *The Fourth World Conference on Faith and Order, Montreal 1963* (Faith and Order Paper No. 42, ed. P.C. Rodger and L. Vischer, SCM Press, London, 1964, pp. 50-60); for the sake of easy reference, the numbering in paragraphs of that publication is maintained here.

* * *

Introduction

38. We find ourselves together in Montreal, delegates of churches with many different backgrounds and many different histories. And yet despite these differences we find that we are able to meet one another in faith and

hope in the one Father, who by his Son Jesus Christ has sent the Holy Spirit to draw all men into unity with one another and with him. It is on the basis of this faith and hope, and in the context of a common prayer to the one God, Father, Son and Holy Spirit, that we have studied together anew the problem of the one Tradition and the many traditions, and despite the fact of our separations, have found that we can talk with one another and grow in mutual understanding.

39. In our report we have distinguished between a number of different meanings of the word *tradition*. We speak of the *Tradition* (with a capital "T"), *tradition* (with a small "t") and *traditions*. By the *Tradition* is meant the Gospel itself, transmitted from generation to generation in and by the Church, Christ himself present in the life of the Church. By *tradition* is meant the traditionary process. The term *traditions* is used in two senses, to indicate both the diversity of forms of expression and also what we call confessional traditions, for instance the Lutheran tradition or the Reformed tradition. In the latter part of our report the word appears in a further sense, when we speak of cultural traditions.

40. Our report contains the substance of the work of three sub-sections. The first considered the subject of the relation of Tradition to Scripture, regarded as the written prophetic and apostolic testimony to God's act in Christ, whose authority we all accept. The concern of the second was with the problem of the one Tradition and the many traditions of Christendom as they unfold in the course of the Church's history. The third discussed the urgent problems raised both in the life of the younger churches and in the churches of the West, concerning the translation of Christian Tradition into new cultures and languages.

41. Part I received a full discussion and the complete approval of the Section. Owing to the lack of time it was not possible to give the same detailed attention to Parts II and III. The Section in general recommends them for study.

I. Scripture, Tradition and traditions

42. As Christians we all acknowledge with thankfulness that God has revealed himself in the history of the people of God in the Old Testament and in Christ Jesus, his Son, the mediator between God and man. God's mercy and God's glory are the beginning and end of our own history. The testimony of prophets and apostles inaugurated the Tradition of his revelation. The once-for-all disclosure of God in Jesus Christ inspired the apostles and disciples to give witness to the revelation given in the person and work of Christ. No one could, and no one can, "say that Jesus is Lord, save by the Holy Spirit" (I Cor. 12:3). The oral and written tradition of the prophets and

apostles under the guidance of the Holy Spirit led to the formation of scriptures and to the canonization of the Old and New Testaments as the Bible of the Church. The very fact that Tradition precedes the scriptures points to the significance of tradition, but also to the Bible as the treasure of the Word of God.

43. The Bible poses the problem of Tradition and Scripture in a more or less implicit manner; the history of Christian theology points to it explicitly. While in the Early Church the relation was not understood as problematical, ever since the Reformation "Scripture and Tradition" has been a matter of controversy in the dialogue between Roman Catholic and Protestant theology. On the Roman Catholic side, tradition has generally been understood as divine truth not expressed in Holy Scripture alone, but orally transmitted. The Protestant position has been an appeal to Holy Scripture alone, as the infallible and sufficient authority in all matters pertaining to salvation, to which all human traditions should be subjected. The voice of the Orthodox Church has hardly been heard in these western discussions until quite recently.

44. For a variety of reasons, it has now become necessary to reconsider these positions. We are more aware of our living in various confessional traditions, e.g. that stated paradoxically in the saying: "It has been the tradition of my church not to attribute any weight to tradition." Historical study and not least the encounter of the churches in the ecumenical movement have led us to realize that the proclamation of the Gospel is always inevitably historically conditioned. We are also aware that in Roman Catholic theology the concept of tradition is undergoing serious reconsideration.

45. In our present situation, we wish to reconsider the problem of Scripture and Tradition, or rather that of Tradition and Scripture. And therefore we wish to propose the following statement as a fruitful way of reformulating the question. Our starting-point is that we are all living in a tradition which goes back to our Lord and has its roots in the Old Testament, and are all indebted to that tradition inasmuch as we have received the revealed truth, the Gospel, through its being transmitted from one generation to another. Thus we can say that we exist as Christians by the Tradition of the Gospel (the *paradosis* of the *kerygma*) testified in Scripture, transmitted in and by the Church through the power of the Holy Spirit. Tradition taken in this sense is actualized in the preaching of the Word, in the administration of sacraments and worship, in Christian teaching and theology, and in mission and witness to Christ by the lives of the members of the Church.

46. What is transmitted in the process of tradition is the Christian faith, not only as a sum of tenets, but as a living reality transmitted through the

operation of the Holy Spirit. We can speak of the Christian Tradition (with a capital "T"), whose content is God's revelation and self-giving in Christ, present in the life of the Church.

47. But this Tradition which is the work of the Holy Spirit is embodied in traditions (in the two senses of the word, both as referring to diversity in forms of expression, and in the sense of separate communions). The traditions in Christian history are distinct from, and yet connected with, the Tradition. They are the expressions and manifestations in diverse historical forms of the one truth and reality which is Christ.

48. This evaluation of the traditions poses serious problems. For some, questions such as these are raised. Is it possible to determine more precisely what the content of the one Tradition is, and by what means? Do all traditions which claim to be Christian contain the Tradition? How can we distinguish between traditions embodying the true Tradition and merely human traditions? Where do we find the genuine Tradition, and where impoverished tradition or even distortion of tradition? Tradition can be faithful transmission of the Gospel, but also a distortion of it. In this ambiguity the seriousness of the problem of tradition is indicated.

49. These questions imply the search for a criterion. This has been a main concern for the Church since its beginning. In the New Testament we find warnings against false teaching and deviations from the truth of the Gospel. For the post-apostolic Church the appeal to the Tradition received from the apostles became the criterion. As this Tradition was embodied in the apostolic writings, it became natural to use those writings as an authority for determining where the true Tradition was to be found. In the midst of all tradition, these early records of divine revelation have a special basic value, because of their apostolic character. But the gnostic crisis in the second century shows that the mere existence of apostolic writings did not solve the problem. The question of interpretation arose as soon as the appeal to written documents made its appearance. When the canon of the New Testament had been finally defined and recognized by the Church, it was still more natural to use this body of writings as an indispensable criterion.

50. The Tradition in its written form, as Holy Scripture (comprising both the Old and the New Testament), has to be interpreted by the Church in ever new situations. Such interpretation of the Tradition is to be found in the crystallization of tradition in the creeds, the liturgical forms of the sacraments and other forms of worship, and also in the preaching of the Word and in the theological expositions of the Church's doctrine. A mere reiteration of the words of Holy Scripture would be a betrayal of the Gospel which has to be made understandable and has to convey a challenge to the world.

51. The necessity of interpretation raises again the question of the criterion for the genuine Tradition. Throughout the history of the Church the criterion has been sought in the holy scriptures rightly interpreted. But what is "right interpretation"?

52. The scriptures as documents can be letter only. It is the Spirit who is the Lord and Giver of life. Accordingly we may say that the right interpretation (taking the words in the widest possible sense) is that interpretation which is guided by the Holy Spirit. But this does not solve the problem of criterion. We arrive at the quest for a hermeneutical principle.

53. This problem has been dealt with in different ways by the various churches. In some confessional traditions the accepted hermeneutical principle has been that any portion of Scripture is to be interpreted in the light of Scripture as a whole. In others the key has been sought in what is considered to be the centre of Holy Scripture, and the emphasis has been primarily on the incarnation, or on the atonement and redemption, or on justification by faith, or again on the message of the nearness of the Kingdom of God, or on the ethical teachings of Jesus. In yet others, all emphasis is laid upon what Scripture says to the individual conscience, under the guidance of the Holy Spirit. In the Orthodox Church the hermeneutical key is found in the mind of the Church, especially as expressed in the Fathers of the Church and in the ecumenical councils. In the Roman Catholic Church the key is found in the deposit of faith, of which the Church's magisterium is the guardian. In other traditions again the creeds, complemented by confessional documents or by the definitions of ecumenical councils and the witness of the Fathers, are considered to give the right key to the understanding of Scripture. In none of these cases where the principle of interpretation is found elsewhere than in Scripture is the authority thought to be alien to the central concept of Holy Scripture. On the contrary, it is considered as providing just a key to the understanding of what is said in Scripture.

54. Loyalty to our confessional understanding of Holy Scripture produces both convergence and divergence in the interpretation of Scripture. For example, an Anglican and a Baptist will certainly agree on many points when they interpret Holy Scripture (in the wide sense of interpretation), but they will disagree on others. As another example, there may be mentioned the divergent interpretations given to Matt. 16:18 in Roman Catholic theology on the one hand, and in Orthodox or Protestant theology on the other. How can we overcome the situation in which we all read Scripture in the light of our own traditions?

55. Modern biblical scholarship has already done much to bring the different churches together by conducting them towards the Tradition. It is

along this line that the necessity for further thinking about the hermeneutical problem arises: i.e. how we can reach an adequate interpretation of the scriptures, so that the Word of God addresses us and Scripture is safeguarded from subjective or arbitrary exegesis. Should not the very fact that God has blessed the Church with the scriptures demand that we emphasize more than in the past a common study of Scripture whenever representatives of the various churches meet? Should we not study more the Fathers of all periods of the Church and their interpretations of the scriptures in the light of our ecumenical task? Does not the ecumenical situation demand that we search for the Tradition by re-examining sincerely our own particular traditions?

II. The unity of Tradition and the diversity of traditions

56. Church and tradition are inseparable. By tradition we do not mean traditionalism. The Tradition of the Church is not an object which we possess, but a reality by which we are possessed. The Church's life has its source in God's act of revelation in Jesus Christ, and in the gift of the Holy Spirit to his people and his work in their history. Through the action of the Holy Spirit, a new community, the Church, is constituted and commissioned, so that the revelation and the life which are in Jesus Christ may be transmitted to the ends of the earth and to the end of time. The Tradition in its content not only looks backward to its origin in the past but also forward to the fullness which shall be revealed. The life of the Church is lived in the continuous recalling, appropriation and transmission of the once-for-all event of Christ's coming in the flesh, and in the eager expectation of his coming in glory. All this finds expression in the Word and in the sacraments in which ''we proclaim the Lord's death till He come'' (I Cor. 11:26).

57. There are at least two distinctive types of understanding of the Tradition. Of these, the first is affirmed most clearly by the Orthodox. For them, the Tradition is not only the act of God in Christ, who comes by the work of the Holy Spirit to save all men who believe in him; it is also the Christian faith itself, transmitted in wholeness and purity, and made explicit in unbroken continuity through definite events in the life of the catholic and apostolic Church from generation to generation. For some others, the Tradition is substantially the same as the revelation in Christ and the preaching of the Word, entrusted to the Church which is sustained in being by it, and expressed with different degrees of fidelity in various historically conditioned forms, namely the traditions. There are others whose understanding of the Tradition and the traditions contains elements of both these points of view. Current developments in biblical and historical study, and the experience of

ecumenical encounter, are leading many to see new values in positions which they had previously ignored. The subject remains open.

58. In the two distinctive positions mentioned above, the Tradition and the traditions are clearly distinguished. But while in the one case it is held that it is to be found in the organic and concrete unity of the one Church, in the other it is assumed that the one Tradition can express itself in a variety of forms, not necessarily all equally complete. The problem of the many churches and the one Tradition appears very differently from each of those points of view. But though on the one side it is possible to maintain that the Church cannot be, and has not been, divided, and on the other to envisage the existence of many churches sharing in the one Tradition even though not in communion with each other, none would wish to acquiesce in the present state of separation.

59. Many of our misunderstandings and disagreements on this subject arise out of the fact of our long history of estrangement and division. During the centuries the different Christian communions have developed their own traditions of historical study and their own particular ways of viewing the past. The rise of the idea of a strictly scientific study of history, with its spirit of accuracy and objectivity, in some ways ameliorated this situation. But the resultant work so frequently failed to take note of the deeper theological issues involved in church history, that its value was severely limited. More recently, a study of history which is ecumenical in its scope and spirit has appeared.

60. We believe that if such a line of study is pursued, it can be of great relevance to the present life and problems of the church: "Those who fail to comprehend their histories are doomed to re-enact them" (Santayana). We believe, too, that it would have great value in offering possibilities of a new understanding of some of the most contested areas of our common past. We therefore specifically recommend that Faith and Order should seek to promote such studies, ensuring the collaboration of scholars of different confessions, in an attempt to gain a new view of crucial epochs and events in church history, especially those in which discontinuity is evident.

61. But at this point another problem arises. At a moment when mankind is becoming ever more aware of itself as a unity, and we are faced with the development of a global civilization, Christians are called to a new awareness of the universality of the Church, and of its history in relation to the history of mankind. This means that, both at the level of theological study and of pastoral teaching, an attempt has to be made to overcome the parochialism of most studies in church history, and to convey some idea of the history of God's people as a whole. But how is this to be done? Does it not demand the

work of historians with more than human capabilities? Is it possible for the scholar, limited as he is by his own cultural, historical and ecclesiastical background, to achieve this vision? Clearly it is not, though we believe that by working in collaboration something could be accomplished. For specialized but limited insights and points of view can be checked and supplemented by those of others; for example, a group may command a larger number of languages and literatures than is possible for an individual. Questions are being raised in the philosophy and theology of history, pointing both to the danger of mere traditionalism and the permanent value of authentic traditionalism. These demand our constant consideration.

62. Still a third kind of historical concern has been with us. We are aware that during the period of this conference we have been passing through a new and unprecedented experience in the ecumenical movement. For the first time in the Faith and Order dialogue, the Eastern Orthodox and the other Eastern Churches have been strongly represented in our meetings. A new dimension of Faith and Order has opened up, and we only begin to see its future possibilities. It is clear that many of our problems of communication have arisen from the inadequate understanding of the life and history of the Eastern Churches to be found even among scholars in the West, and vice versa. Here again is an area in which we would recommend further study, e.g. of the problem of the *filioque*, its origin and consequences. There are two other studies which we recommend to the Faith and Order Commission. We believe it important to undertake together a study of the councils of the Early Church, and we recommend an examination of the catechetical material at present in use by the churches, and of the methods whereby it could be revised in the light of the ecumenical movement.

63. In all this we are not blind to the nature of the world in which we live, nor to the cultural and intellectual problems of our day. To many of our contemporaries a concern with the past will immediately appear suspect, as revealing a desire for the mere resuscitation of old customs and ideas, which have no relevance for the urgent questions of our time. We recognize that in many places human traditions — national, social, and indeed religious — are being shaken; and that in this age of scientific and technological achievement many tend to regard the heritage of the past as unimportant. We recognize the positive elements in the present situation. It is for this reason that we have placed the contrast of tradition and traditionalism at the beginning of this part. The past of which we speak is not only a subject which we study from afar. It is a past which has value for us, in so far as we make it our own in an act of personal decision. In the Church it becomes a past by which we live by

sharing in the one Tradition, for in it we are united with him who is the Lord of history, who was and is and is to come; and He is God not of the dead but of the living.

III. The Christian Tradition and cultural diversity

64. In what has been written so far, we have been concerned primarily with the understanding of Tradition as it relates to the past, to the once-for-all event of Christ's coming in the flesh, his death and resurrection, and to the continuing work of the Holy Spirit within the Church. But we have recognized throughout that Tradition looks also to the present and to the future. The Church is sent by Christ to proclaim the Gospel to all men; the Tradition must be handed on in time and also in space. In other words, Tradition has a vital missionary dimension in every land, for the command of the Lord is to go to all nations. Whatever differences of interpretation there may be, all are agreed that there is this dynamic element in the Tradition, which comes from the action of God within the history of his people and its fulfilment in the person and work of Christ, and which looks to the consummation of the victory of the Lord at the end of time.

65. The problems raised by the transmission of the Tradition in different lands and cultures, and by the diversities of traditions in which the one Tradition has been transmitted, are common in varying ways to all Christians. They are to be seen in an acute form in the life of the younger churches of Asia and Africa today, and in a less obvious but no less real form in what was formerly called western Christendom. To take the problem of the younger churches, in one quite small and typical country there are more than eighty different denominations. How among these traditions are we to find the Tradition? In the building up of new nations there is a particular need for all that will make for unity among men. Are Christians, to whom the ministry of reconciliation has been committed, to be a factor of division at such a time? It is in such testing circumstances as these that the serious problems have to be faced of how the Church may become truly indigenous, bringing into the service of Christ all that is good in the life of every culture and nation, without falling into syncretism.

66. When the Word became flesh, the Gospel came to man through a particular cultural medium, that of the Palestinian world of the time. So when the Church takes the Tradition to new peoples, it is necessary that again the essential content should find expression in terms of new cultures. Thus in the great missionary expansion of the Eastern Church, the Tradition was transmitted through the life of the Church into new languages and cultures,

such as those of Russia and the other mission fields. Just as the use of the Slavonic tongue was necessary for the transmission of the Tradition to the Slavs, so today it is necessary to use new languages and new forms of expression which can be understood by those to whom the good news comes. In order that this can be rightly done, it is necessary to draw together knowledge of the culture and language in question, along with a careful study of the languages of the Old and New Testaments, and a thorough knowledge of Church history. It is in this context that we begin to understand the meaning of the gift of tongues at Pentecost. By the power of the Holy Spirit the apostles were enabled to preach the mighty works of God to each man in his own tongue, and thus the diversity of nations and cultures was united in the service of God. Through recognizing this, Christians in countries where they are a small minority can avoid the dangers of developing a "ghetto mentality".

67. The content of the Tradition cannot be exactly defined, for the reality it transmits can never be fully contained in propositional forms. In the Orthodox view, Tradition includes an understanding of the events recorded in the New Testament, of the writings of the Fathers, of the ecumenical creeds and Councils, and of the life of the Church throughout the centuries. All member churches of the World Council of Churches are united in confessing the Lord Jesus Christ "as God and Saviour, according to the Scriptures, and in seeking together to fulfil their common calling to the glory of the one God, Father, Son and Holy Spirit". This basis of membership safeguards a position from which we may seek constantly to grow in understanding of the fullness of God's revelation, and to correct partial apprehensions of the truth. In the task of seeking to understand the relation between the Tradition and the traditions, problems are raised as difficult to solve as they are crucial in importance. Such questions often cannot be answered apart from the specific situations which pose them. There are no ready-made solutions. Yet some things may be said.

68. What is basic in the Old and New Testament record and interpretation remains basic for the Church in any situation. Moreover, the Holy Spirit has been given to the Church to guide it into all truth. The decisions which communities of God's believing people have to take are to be made in reliance on this leading of his Spirit within the Church, and in awareness of God's providential operations in the world. In the process of indigenization (understood in its widest sense), nothing can be admitted which is at variance with the good news of what God has done, is doing and will do, in the redemption of the world through our Lord Jesus Christ, as expressed in terms of the Church's christocentric and trinitarian faith. In each particular

situation, the Gospel should be so proclaimed that it will be experienced, not as a burdensome law, but as a "joyful, liberating and reconciling power". The Church must be careful to avoid all unnecessary offence in the proclamation of its message, but the offence of the cross itself, as foolishness to the world, can never be denied. And so the attempt must always be made to transmit the Tradition in its fullness and to remain within the community of the whole of God's people, and the temptation must be avoided of over-emphasizing those elements which are especially congenial to a particular culture. It is in the wholeness of God's truth that the Church will be enabled to fulfil its mission and to bear authentic witness.

69. The traditionary process involves the dialectic, both of relating the Tradition as completely as possible to every separate cultural situation in which men live, and at the same time of demonstrating its transcendence of all that divides men from one another. From this comes the truth that the more the Tradition is expressed in the varying terms of particular cultures, the more will its universal character be fully revealed. It is only "with all the saints" that we come to know the fullness of Christ's love and glory (Eph. 3:18-19).

70. Catholicity, as a gift of God's grace, calls us to a task. It is a concept of immense richness whose definition is not attempted here. It can be sought and received only through consciousness of, and caring for, the wholeness of Christ's body, through witness for Christ's lordship over every area of human life, and through compassionate identification with every man in his own particular need.

71. In the fulfilment of their missionary task most churches claim not merely to be reproducing themselves, but in some sense to be planting the *una sancta ecclesia*. Surely this fact has implications which are scarcely yet realized, let alone worked out, both for the life of the mother churches, and also for all that is involved in the establishing of any new church in an ecumenical age. It demands that the liberty of newly-founded churches be recognized, so that both mother and daughter churches may receive together the one gift of God's grace. This demands faithfulness to the whole *koinonia* of Christ's Church, even when we are engaged with particular problems. In this connection we recognize a vital need for the study of the history of the Church's life and mission, written from an ecumenical perspective. All must labour together in seeking to receive and manifest the fullness of Christ's truth.

72. The problem of communicating this fullness of truth today is felt throughout the whole modern world. This is a result of the emergence in our time of a global civilization, shaped by rapid technological advances, and grounded in a scientific outlook that transforms our concept of the universe.

The new cosmology which is taking shape challenges our traditional conceptions of man and of nature, both in themselves and in their inter-relationship with one another. Amid these developments, and to some degree because of them, radical changes in social structure are taking place in every part of the world. The Church is thus faced with a dual responsibility. The Tradition has to be simultaneously transmitted in diverse ways; on the one hand, in popular everyday language; on the other hand, in terms of the most complex and critical contemporary thought. The seriousness of this revolutionary situation cannot easily be exaggerated. We have seen its inherent dangers, but we must equally seek to realize its enormous potentialities for good.

73. Our thinking about the Christian faith too often lacks a forward-looking vision and orientation. The phrase *in partibus infidelium* has already acquired a universal reference. Experiments in pastoral and evangelistic work, such as industrial chaplaincies and "store front parishes", are first attempts at meeting this need. The deepest witness is always borne by the life of the Church itself, through its prayer and sacramental worship, and through the bearing of the cross in silence. As we address ourselves together to our common problems, we may find that God is using the pressures of the world to break the barriers which divide us from one another. We must recognize the opportunity given to us, and with vigour and boldness fulfil the Church's great commission to transmit the Tradition, the word of grace and hope, to men in this new global culture, as in the past it was preached to Jerusalem, to Hellas, Rome and Gaul, and to the uttermost parts of the earth.

3. The Significance of the Hermeneutical Problem for the Ecumenical Movement

The Fourth World Conference on Faith and Order in Montreal (1963) had called for a clarification of the problems of biblical exegesis and interpretation. So the Faith and Order secretariat, in collaboration with the Division of Studies, organized a preparatory consultation on these problems at Bad Schauenburg near Basle in 1964. The chairman of the consultation, Prof. Erich Dinkler, reported to the Commission on the discussion and submitted an outline for a study on the subject (Aarhus Minutes, Faith and Order Paper No. 44, Geneva, 1965, pp. 61-69). At its meeting in Aarhus (1964), the Faith and Order Commission authorized the study on the hermeneutical problem.

Subsequently, five regional groups were formed: one in Germany/The Netherlands, one in Britain, two in the United States and one in France/Switzerland. Each group was asked to study certain passages of the Bible and to analyse the hermeneutical principles used in the course of its exegesis and interpretation.

In spring 1967, the five groups sent in their findings (group reports in WCC archives, FO/67:20), which were summarized and analysed by Prof. James Barr (WCC archives FO/67:25). At a concluding meeting in Heidelberg, at which two representatives of each group were present, the final report was drawn up. It was presented to the Faith and Order Commission at its meeting in Bristol (1967) and afterwards published in *New Directions in Faith and Order, Bristol, 1967* (Faith and Order Paper No. 50, Geneva, 1968, pp. 32-41).

*   *
*

THE HERMENEUTICAL PROCESS

I. Introduction

There is a generally accepted process of scholarly exegesis which is the practice of biblical scholars, upon which the Church is to a considerable extent dependent and to which it is deeply indebted. It is not easy to give a full description of this process, for it is a complex one; but what follows is an attempt to point out some of the methods which it employs and the reasons for them. These methods are not rules in the sense that, if they are followed, they will certainly bring us to the right results; it may be possible for important results to be achieved even when they are ignored. But it can be said that, generally speaking, they are the methods used in the best scholarly exegesis, and that interpretation which is not based upon them has to be regarded with greater caution. In this sense they may be taken as rules.

The Bible contains a group of literary documents, and it has to be studied by the same methods as are used in the study of other literary documents. Any passage in the Bible has to be investigated for its meaning within both wider and narrower contexts. The narrower context may be a single story, passage, or chapter. The wider context may be, for example, the whole work of one biblical writer or the whole of one biblical book, or even a genre of biblical books such as the wisdom or apocalyptic literature. A passage has also to be related, where possible, to the situation in the life of Israel or the Church in which it was being used. We therefore hold that the literary-critical method is a necessary one.

The Bible is in many of its parts the product of a historical process. It came into being through historical events and experiences, and through reflection upon them. Traditions and writings were handed down in Israel and in the Early Church, and were often in the course of long periods combined, reworked and reinterpreted in the light of later historical situations. It is therefore necessary for a full understanding of the present text to trace this historical process. In doing this we may find layer upon layer of tradition; each of these layers has a particular historical background which has to be discerned for the full understanding of it. We therefore hold that the historical-critical method is a necessary one.

II. Unity and diversity

The Bible contains a collection of very diverse literary traditions, the contents of which often stand in tension with one another. The diversity constitutes one of the main problems for the theological understanding of the Bible. Sometimes the diversities can be understood as providing complementary aspects of the truth, but sometimes, as far as we can see, there may be real contradictions. Where positions are complementary, they indicate the richness of biblical truth. Where they are, as far as we can see, really contradictory, this may go back to real theological disagreements within the biblical period itself or it may have been occasioned by different social or historical situations. The difficulties raised by this for systematic theology have not been solved by us.

(The particularistic tradition, for instance, of Ezra and the universalism of some of the prophets, or the different conception of ecclesiastical offices in Paul and the "Deutero-Pauline" letters may be seen as, in a certain way, complementary. On the other hand, the concept of providence in Chronicles and the book of Job, or the way in which the future of Israel is conceived in I Thess. 2:14-16 and in Rom. 11:25 ff. are, so far as we can see, contradictory. Even christological statements in the NT are sometimes in tension: compare e.g. Rom. 1:3 f. and Matt. 1:8 ff. and John 1:1 ff.).

It is important that diversities and contradictions should not be glossed over. Though theology must in the end strive to present an overall picture of biblical truth, it is essential that forced harmonization be avoided. Only after texts have been examined for what they say in themselves may we go on to build a composite structure from them in combination or even to decide for this or against that concept. This applies both to systematic theology and to the practical use of the Bible in the Church.

The diversity of thought within the Bible reflects the diversity of God's actions in different historical situations and the diversity of human response to God's actions. It is important that the scholar should not attach himself to one facet of biblical thought, however central it seems to him to be, in such a way as to cut himself off from this variety and richness. Although the truth in Christ is one, the human witness to it is manifold.

There is a diversity of church traditions which in some of its aspects may be related to that diversity of traditions already found in the Bible, to which we have referred in the earlier part of our report. In that case the quest for unity between these church traditions will involve the appropriation of the unity of the Gospel as it is reflected in the plurality of the individual biblical witnesses.

It is dangerous to quote isolated texts as "proof texts" as has often been done. Small literary units cannot be rightly used without testing and checking their functions as parts of larger complexes. There are, however, certain sentences which, after testing for congruence with the tendency of larger units, prove to be good summaries or epitomies of significant thoughts, and it is then legitimate to cite them as such.

III. The process of interpretation

THE ORIGINAL TEXT

The earliest form of the biblical text must be established as carefully and accurately as possible. The text of the Bible itself has undergone a historical transmission, and the original autographs no longer exist. It is therefore essential that the textual history be carefully scrutinized, and that exegesis be done with an awareness of it. Later textual developments should not necessarily be disregarded and may have real importance, for they may indicate ways in which the material of the earlier text-form was interpreted.

(In Luke 2:27, 33, 41, 43, 48 Joseph is spoken of as the father of Jesus. In the textual variants the words "father" and "parents" are changed, an indication that these words were felt to be offensive in view of Mary's virginity.)

CONCERNING NEW TRANSLATIONS

Scholarly interpretation of the Bible depends on knowledge of the languages in which the Bible was written, basically Hebrew and Greek. No translation, e.g. Vulgate, King James Version or Luther's, has final authority, and new translations have to be made from time to time, for instance, because of (i) progress in textual criticism, (ii) changes in the meanings of words, and (iii) changes in the way in which the work of translation is conceived. The diversity of new translations and of the cultural environments in which they are produced, however, only makes clearer the necessity of the original text and language as a meeting point for all scholars. We therefore recommend that every church should have within it an adequate number of people who have real contact with the original languages.

(One of the reasons why churches today may ask for new translations is that they want them made across denominational lines. We warmly acclaim and specially recommend this, because we are convinced that it can help the ecumenical cause.)

MEANING AND MEANINGS

In dealing with a passage, a distinction is often made between "historical" and "unhistorical" or between "genuine" and "unauthentic" elements. Though this is, as scholarship recognizes, a debatable and ambiguous terminology and perhaps better to be discarded, it is one which points to a necessary distinction. This should not, however, involve a value judgment, such as to suggest that only the "historical" or the "genuine" can be used with confidence. The "unhistorical" may illuminate the "historical", the "unauthentic" passage may provide a useful complement to, or interpretation of, the "authentic".

(In the story of the sending of spies into Canaan, the "unhistorical" exaggeration of the size of the grapes, Numbers 13:24, glorifies God's promised land. The "unhistorical" adoration of the Wise Men in Matthew 2 points to the universal significance of Christ.)

When scholarship discerns several layers in a document or passage — some of which may be from a primitive or pre-literary stage while others are carefully and reflectively developed, and yet others are late glosses or additions — it must work on all of these layers, since any or all of them may be theologically relevant. Each layer may indicate how an earlier one was later understood, and thus a passage may have not only one meaning but several meanings.

(E.g. the later cultic redaction of particular individual psalms or the promises of salvation added later on to the threats in Deuteronomy and to the pronouncements of judgment in the prophets. See also the question of sacraments and eschatology in the fourth gospel.)

Even when there are not different layers of this kind, it may be necessary to recognize that some texts have a plurality of meanings rather than one only. We should therefore be cautious before speaking about "the meaning" of a passage.

(E.g. the parable of the Prodigal Son as it now stands in Luke 15:11-32 can have several points or "meanings", such as the sin and repentance of the younger son, the forgiveness and loving-kindness of the father, his joy, the attitude of the older son and the relation between the two brothers. One should not say that one of these is *the* point the story wants to make.)

The Bible makes extensive use of imagery and symbols. The thoughts expressed thereby are sometimes such that they cannot be stated in other terms than images and symbols, and it may be a distortion if we try to express the sense of them in conceptual terms. Conceptual terms may make the sense too narrow and precise. On the other hand, the use of symbolic language can be uncontrolled, and a comparative study of the widespread use of a particular symbol in different cultures may help to bring to light what is basic and essential in it, and so make possible its appropriation by modern man.

(E.g. the blood in expressions as "redemption" or "justification" through "the blood of Christ" is a symbol which, if taken literally, denotes a magical conception. This blood-symbol in the New Testament can be compared with its occurrence in other religions in order to uncover a common denominator in the various usages of it and thus what the basic intention of this symbol is.)

Scholarly exegesis has to concern itself with the details and minutiae of the Bible, because these are essential for the import of the larger complexes. Understanding requires a balanced appreciation of the inter-relation between the whole of a text and its parts, between the minutiae of each element and the impact or effect of the whole. It is often the case that sympathetic insight is gained through the study of minutiae.

SECULAR SCHOLARSHIP

A great part of the process as thus described, or indeed most of it could be carried out equally by Christians and non-Christians. While the personal involvement of Christians helps them to see the theological depths of meaning in the text, it is also true that love can make us blind. The detachment of non-Christians can be creative and constructive.

Forms of knowledge other than the theological can be of much service in the study of the Bible. For instance, some of the exegetical "rules" stated above are reinforced by comparison with some of the methods used in the study of secular literature. Literary appreciation asserts that the part makes sense only when seen against the background of the whole, and that the relationship of a passage to the whole text brings out new meanings which are not apparent if a passage is viewed in isolation. We therefore suggest that biblical study should take account of the work done by interpreters of other kinds of literature. We would also want to point to the contributions which history, linguistics and philosophy can make; the biblical exegete should make use of the scholarship of those who work in those fields.

Philosophy has to be mentioned in particular, because the Church not only speaks to the world outside, but receives from the world outside categories of thinking which it must use to understand and express its own message. The conscious study of these categories may enable us to prevent them from becoming dominant in a harmful way, and may also make it possible to translate our thought from one system of philosophical categories into another.

(E.g. those who employ Heideggerian terms to express the Christian message and those who stand in the tradition of the Wittgensteinian school of linguistic analysis or use phenomenological categories often do not understand each other's language. When the philosophical categories are further explained, it sometimes becomes apparent that these groups are expressing the same thought in their different categories, or at least that they are less far apart than they seemed to be at first — though the reverse might also be the case.)

QUESTIONS ARISING OUT OF THE TEXT

The reading of a biblical text (like that of any other) conveys to us a certain initial understanding of its meaning. The task of interpretation is to discuss and elaborate this initial understanding and if necessary to correct it, in order that the text itself may speak to us more profoundly. For this the text itself may suggest to us questions for further penetration into its sense. In using these questions which arise out of the text for a questioning of the text, the following points have to be observed: (i) Not every question which arises will necessarily be suitable or appropriate when rechecked against the text. In that case the question will not deepen our understanding and has to be discarded. (ii) The richness of a passage means that a large variety of possible questions may arise. (iii) The following up of each appropriate question leads to a better understanding of the text from a particular aspect. Since in this process other aspects are necessarily dimmed, each question means at the same time a limitation of our understanding. If the text as a whole is to be understood, it has to be investigated by means of several questions.

(Several legitimate questions are suggested by Rom. 9-11 about the Church and Israel, about election and reprobation, about the righteousness of God, about the tension within Paul as Christian and Jew, about mission, etc.).

QUESTIONS PUT TO THE TEXT

There are also questions which do not so much arise out of the biblical texts themselves, but which we from our side put to the Bible. The more questions were already in the field of vision of the biblical writers, the more direct will be the answers which we receive. When, however, we approach the Bible with questions which come to us from our situation but which were foreign to the writers, the Bible will give us indirect answers, or sometimes no answers at all.

(Many texts give direct answers to the question how the relationship between God and man is to be viewed, but only indirect answers may be given, e.g. about the meaning of work or about sexuality.)

PREVIOUS UNDERSTANDING

All study of the Bible is affected by our previous knowledge and understanding. Without this previous understanding, drawn from past experience or from study and reflection, we would be unable to organize any new insights we received. But this previous understanding, because it leads us to expect certain results to follow, and because it makes us frame our questions in a certain way, is also a source of difficulty and error. This is so both in general scholarly exegesis, where scholarship consists in certain traditions of investigation, and also still more in regard to the use of the Bible for the elucidation or solution of particular ethical or theological problems. Study of the Bible must therefore carry with it the willingness to have our previous understandings called into question and to revise them.

(To understand the meaning of such a sentence as "God loved the world" we must have some previous understanding of what "God", "love", and "world" mean. When the question is asked what the Bible says about the "immortality of the soul", it may appear that the question so put is not appropriate, and that it has to be reformulated in the light of the biblical evidence.)

IV. The Bible and the speech and action of the Church

It has to be kept in mind that the Gospel to which the Bible witnesses founded the Church. The Bible is a given fact in the Church. The life of the Church has always influenced its understanding and, reciprocally, the understanding of the Bible has influenced this life. In order that in the future also the Bible may maintain its salutary hold on the Church, the work of interpretation must go on in as scholarly and careful a manner as possible. However, the relation between biblical exegesis and the speech and action of the Church is an indirect process which cannot be determined by methodological rules. To take the results of exegesis over directly into the teaching and practice of the Church is rarely possible or desirable. But it is important that a continual and recognizable interaction should exist between exegesis done in a responsible manner and the actions of the Church, its worship and its teaching.

SOME GENERAL CONSIDERATIONS

I. To what extent is the hermeneutical process governed by confessional traditions?

In the statement by the Fourth World Conference on Faith and Order the different positions with regard to the relation between Scripture and any interpretation of it were stated largely in terms of existing Christian confessions. In the course of our examination of the question, it has appeared that the situation is more complex, and this complexity could have positive as well as negative consequences. In particular, the following two considerations were put forward.

1. In the course of their exegetical work scholars sometimes discover themselves to be less complete representatives of their confessional standpoints than they had supposed themselves to be, or than when they began. This may come about because in doing exegesis they discover the scriptures to be of such a kind that (a) the validity of other standpoints and principles of interpretation than their own have to be acknowledged as also answering to the character of the scriptures themselves, and (b) they are unable to state their own principles of interpretation in such a way as to establish them as self-evident or conclusive or as superior to all others. Thus, while the diverse nature of the scriptures is of such a kind that any scholar must have some provisional principles of interpretation before he can begin, it is doubtful whether any one interpretative principle can be so stated as to become a prescriptive instrument applicable in all circumstances.

2. It can be that particular aspects of Scripture come to the fore and demand special attention not by reason of a confessional standpoint, not as the result of the application of interpretative principles, but because a particular historical situation has developed, and Christians must speak to it.

II. Tradition, Scripture and the Church

The Montreal Conference used the following formulation: "We can say that we exist as Christians by the Tradition of the Gospel (the *paradosis* of the *kerygma*), testified in Scripture, transmitted in and by the Church through the power of the Holy Spirit."[1] This sentence expresses an agreement which we all can support. It covers, however, different possible positions. In accepting this statement the relationship between Scripture and the Church can still be understood differently depending on the emphasis laid upon the various elements of the sentence. This may especially be the case where it is a question of the relation between what the Bible says and some specific contemporary issue on which it is the duty of the Church to attempt to state its mind.

In the course of exegesis and discussion three positions have emerged which may be stated, though only in summary form, as follows:

1. For some, Scripture is to be regarded as the sole norm of truth on which the Church is entirely dependent. To know the truth Christians are to have

---

[1] *The Fourth World Conference on Faith and Order: the Report from Montreal 1963*, eds P.C. Rodger and L. Vischer. New York: Association Press, 1964, p. 52, paragraph 45.

recourse exclusively to this primary testimony as it has been handed down to them by the Church. The main principles of interpretation, however difficult to discover or to state, will be dictated by Scripture itself. Exegesis, interpretation, and application of the Scripture are therefore of decisive importance for establishing the Christian witness today, though in such application the statements of Scripture are not necessarily to be taken over directly and without translation, and on some issues it might have little or nothing to say.

2. Some would rather emphasize that Scripture is the product of the same tradition which has had a continuous life in the Church. It is its verbal expression, but it does not contain the full truth. It needs to be read in the context of the general Christian tradition, which apart from Scripture finds expression in sacraments, creeds, Christian thinking and cultural values indirectly derived from Scripture. The interpretation of Scripture according to hermeneutical rules is a necessary part of the Church's task, since its life and thinking are to be "consonant with Scripture" (however that may be defined), but it is carried out in the context of the whole life of the Church. The truth of Scripture will not be the sum total of the results of exegeses, since these will only be incorporated into Christian life and discourse through the medium of a particular form of Christian tradition and practice.

3. Still others would emphasize that Scripture is only one element in a variegated complex of Christian truth. It accompanies the life of the Church, and must be taken into account along with other factors through which truth is mediated, such as the evolution of human thought, cultural development, what the churches have made out of the biblical outlook, and perhaps much else besides. That the biblical text should be the starting point for the discussion of any issue is not simply to be taken for granted, but must be argued for in each instance. Preaching, dogmatic theology, and Church pronouncements should be concerned with what Christians are to believe now, and while in arriving at this the tradition of the Church will be important, and Scripture will always have a vital place as expressing the mind of the Church when still within the orbit of the events from which it took its origin, this does not mean that any particular formulated account or understanding of those events is finally authoritative. The Church is in dialogue with Scripture, but has been fed from many sources, in the light of which biblical statements may have to be declared inadequate, or erroneous, or as "without meaning" except as modified by truth arrived at from these other sources.

None of these positions is held exclusively. They are differing emphases and are to be seen in relation to each other. In practice, however, they may lead to different conclusions. The following questions may indicate their inter-relation:

1. Do those who stress the exclusive authority of scriptures really derive their insight from this only source?

2. How do those speaking of the life of the Church identify the Christian truth?

3. How is the distinction to be made between elements in Christian history which reveal God's truth and those which do not?

III. Diversity in the Bible and the ecumenical movement

The present development of hermeneutics has a particular impact on the prospects of the ecumenical movement, especially as it is represented in the World Council of Churches. When the World Council of Churches was founded, there was a strong hope, confirmed by facts, that in the different churches and theological schools the Bible would be read more and more along the same lines, provided by the development of the so-called "biblical theology" of that period. In its main trend this conceived of the Bible as unity, whose centre was the divine acts of salvation interpreted by a more or less harmonious community of witnesses. It found in the Bible a common message which seemed to throw light upon all kinds of problems with which modern man had to wrestle.

Now, two decades later, attention is increasingly drawn to the diversity amongst or even contradiction between biblical writers. Scholars investigate the different "setting in life" of the different writings and the correspondent different interpretations of salvation. As a consequence the hope that the churches would find themselves to have in the near future the basis of a common understanding of the one biblical message has been fading, even to such an extent that in the eyes of some the new exegetical developments seem to undermine the raison d'être of the ecumenical movement.

However, these developments may also contribute to a deeper understanding of unity. Of course, the differences between our churches are only partly due to differences in understanding the Gospel. Non-theological factors are often more dominant than the hermeneutical differences. But insofar as our confessional divisions are related to different reading of the scriptures the hermeneutical debate helps us to see that similar differences are already present within the canonical books themselves. The awareness of the differences within the Bible will lead us towards a deeper understanding of our divisions and will help us to interpret them more readily as possible and legitimate interpretations of one and the same Gospel.

Thus the fact that biblical scholars are studying the problems of diversity and unity at a deeper level than before may prove to be a significant step for the ecumenical movement and it may be one of the important theological tasks to draw the right conclusions from the insight that the biblical canon itself bears witness to unity and diversity at the very beginning of the Church.

4. The Authority of the Bible

The Faith and Order Commission, having received the report on the hermeneutical problem, decided to undertake a study on the authority of the Bible (Bristol 1967).

The study process was initiated by a consultation of twenty-five theologians at Boldern, near Zürich, in October 1968. The conference decided not to embark immediately on a systematic reflection on the authority of the Bible, but to begin with the exegesis of biblical texts on specific themes. What authority do these texts actually have? In what way do they authoritatively illumine the themes? Only after an attempt at answering these questions was the general issue of biblical authority discussed. The findings of the Boldern consultation were summarized by Prof. James Barr in the paper "The Authority of the Bible: a Study Outline" (*The Ecumenical Review*, Vol. XXI, No. 2, 1969, pp. 135-150). Four articles on the concept of authority by Eberhard Jüngel (Lutheran, FRG), Gerhard Krodel (Lutheran, USA), René Marlé, SJ (Roman Catholic, France) and John D. Zizioulas (Orthodox, Greece) were attached to the study outline (*ibid.*, pp. 150-166).

In the light of the outline and appendices, the subject was then studied by a number of groups in various countries: a Dutch-German group, a German group, a British group, two groups in the United States, two French groups, a Spanish group, an Ethiopian group, a Scandinavian group. Most groups produced reports of their findings (WCC archives FO/71:5). A new and significant development was that Roman Catholic theologians participated fully in the initial consultation and were active members in many of the regional study groups.

A summary of the group reports, prepared by Dr Ellen Flesseman-van Leer (WCC archives FO/71:6), served as a working paper for the representatives of the groups who met at Cartigny near Geneva in spring 1971 to draw up the final report of the study. This report was submitted to and accepted by the Faith and Order Commission at its Louvain meeting (1971) and published in *Faith and Order, Louvain 1971*, (Faith and Order Paper No. 59, Geneva, 1971, pp. 9-23).

*   *
*

I. The problem

The question which the study organized by the Faith and Order Commission set out to investigate may be formulated as follows: How far is the Bible authoritative for Christian thought and action? One obvious answer would be that the Bible is authoritative because through it we can hear God's Word and learn his will. But this answer prompts the further question: How are we to approach the Bible so that, through the biblical text, God may speak to us authoritatively today?

To feel the full force of this question we must first realize that the Bible is the common point of reference for all Christians and all churches. It is the basis of their faith and the rule of their conduct. The fact that all churches ultimately test and verify their preaching and teaching by Scripture gives them a common orientation. An intensive study of the Bible has also been typical of the ecumenical movement so far. The study of the scriptures led Christians of different traditions together. In the ecumenical movement they learned to read the Bible with new vision. Their horizon was expanded. It consequently proved possible, without much difficulty, to include a reference to the Bible in the Basis of the World Council of Churches.

But the automatic acceptance of the Bible as basis and standard has in many places been severely shaken of late. Many Christians find the Bible alien to them and to their daily life; they find it increasingly difficult to hear God addressing them directly in the words of the Bible. This difficulty is even felt by many churches. It is only with considerable difficulty that they are able to find in the Bible and its authority a clear basis for their witness and action in the contemporary world. But even in the ecumenical movement a certain perplexity has arisen over the Bible. It turns out that the Bible is read in different ways in the different churches. The Bible is used to justify divergent positions and thus even an appeal to Scripture can itself lead to fresh differences. Above all, difficulties have cropped up as churches have tried to speak and act together on the basis of the Bible. Occasional attempts to call the Christian answer to a specific problem more or less directly from the Bible have proved unsatisfactory. As a result the tendency has been more and more to abandon the appeal to biblical grounds altogether. Thus the problem simply is avoided, which is not a satisfactory course either.

Why do the churches today find it so difficult to speak together authoritatively on the basis of Scripture? What factors compel us to investigate the problem of the authority of the Bible? Three considerations are mentioned here to clarify the situation which is the starting point of this study:

1. CONFESSIONAL DIFFERENCES

We must first consider the confessional factors. The various confessions have different views of the significance of the Bible. Certainly the old controversy over Scripture and Tradition has to a large extent been settled in recent years. The Fourth World Conference on Faith and Order in Montreal was able to record the following consensus: "Thus we can say that we exist as Christians by the Tradition of the Gospel (the *paradosis* of the *kerygma*) testified in Scripture, transmitted in and by the Church through the power of the Holy Spirit" (paragraph 45).[1] Important as this agreement undoubtedly is, it still leaves room for different emphases. We can, for example, emphasize the Bible as the authoritative witness of the Tradition. But equally we can emphasize the importance of the process of tradition in and by the Church. Our treatment of Scripture will depend on which of these emphases we choose. If we choose the first, we shall tend to treat the scriptures as the standard in all questions; if we choose the second, we shall tend to attach more weight to the traditional teaching of the Church. But confessional factors come even more to the forefront when we try to interpret Scripture in contemporary terms. To a far greater extent than we care to admit, the hermeneutical methods employed in the interpretation of Scripture are influenced by the tradition of the individual confessions. The Montreal conference gave examples of this (paragraph 53).[2] Consider, for example, the important role of the tradition of the Ancient Church, in the Orthodox churches, the role of the magisterium in the Roman Catholic Church, or the place of the confessional documents in the Protestant churches, and so on. These confessional peculiarities may seem irrelevant to many, but the fact remains that they influence the thought of the churches in question and predispose them to a certain attitude towards Scripture. Another important factor in this connection is the actual use made of the Bible in the individual churches. It makes a difference if preaching is normally based on the Bible or if it is mainly in the Scripture lessons in the liturgy that the Bible is heard.

---

[1] See *The Fourth World Conference on Faith and Order: the Report from Montreal 1963*, eds P.C. Rodger and L. Vischer. New York: Association Press, 1964, p. 52.
[2] *Op. cit.*, p.53.

2. THE INFLUENCE OF HISTORICAL CRITICISM

It is generally agreed that the Bible must be studied and interpreted as a collection of human documents dating from a specific historical period and in accordance with the procedures adopted for any other literary document of the past. On the basis of historical and critical study, biblical scholarship has in recent decades cleared up many obscurities. While there may still be differences on many matters of detail, the method of enquiry is almost universally accepted and biblical scholars of different confessional traditions often arrive at astonishingly similar exegetical findings. Does historical criticism and its methods therefore represent a unifying factor? Many have entertained this hope. It was expressly affirmed by the Montreal conference: "Modern scholarship has already done much to bring the different churches together by conducting them towards the Tradition" (paragraph 55).[3] This statement is undoubtedly true but its limits must also be recognized. Application of the methods of historical criticism has also brought out more clearly than ever the diversity of the biblical witness. The individual passages and traditions of the Bible are all aligned to specific historical situations and the Bible is the collection of these diverse testimonies. But which of these witnesses is authoritative? For many Christians this question is inevitably associated with fear lest the methods of historical criticism should destroy the authority of the Bible and with it the Christian faith itself. This fear is ultimately baseless. But clearly historical and critical scholarship has resulted in a new encounter with the biblical records and therefore makes a fresh account of biblical authority necessary.

3. HISTORICAL REMOTENESS

Closely bound up with this is the further consideration that critical scholarship has made us keenly aware of the historical character of the biblical witness and consequently of its temporal remoteness from the reader of the Bible today. The message of the Bible is expressed in terms we no longer use. As a document of past history it requires transposition into the present time. For it to become really relevant to us it needs to be expressed in categories appropriate to today. Man's present situation must be taken into account. But clearly men live in very diverse situations. Cultural factors differ from one society to another. People's thinking is influenced by different philosophical traditions. Inevitably the process of transposition takes place in very varied conditions, therefore, and the results cannot be fully in accord.

The question arises: How, in view of this historical gulf, can any relevance be claimed for the Bible at all? This question does not present itself

---

[3] *Op. cit.*, p.54.

everywhere with the same urgency, of course. Even today, many churches and Christians assume almost unquestioningly an attitude of contemporaneity with the Bible and feel no need to attach any great importance to its historical character. It is also possible to adopt a quite sophisticated version of this synchronized view of the Bible and the present-day reader and to insist on it as an alternative to critical scholarship. This happens, for example, where the discoveries and the methods of structuralism are being applied to the exegesis of biblical texts.

But a variety of answers can be given to the question just mentioned even by those who are aware of the problem of historical remoteness. Some hold that, as God's Word, the Bible has a timeless claim on every generation and that its message can speak directly to the men of all times provided it is set free from the historically conditioned forms in which it is clothed. Man with his questions remains fundamentally the same and, since the Bible answers his deepest questions, it is still relevant for today. But others believe that God's action in history to which the Bible bears witness continues further and that the present situation is primarily to be understood not as analogous to that earlier time but as its fruit. Which of these general conceptions we adopt will determine our reading of the Bible and our interpretation of its message.

II. The concept of authority

What do we mean when we speak of the "authority" of Scripture? The term can be used in a number of ways and we must be clear about these various meanings from the outset.

1. In the first place, the Bible has a certain weight as a literary document. When people — Christians and non-Chistians alike — read this document and seek to understand it, in a certain sense they "submit" themselves to this authority. This applies to the reading and interpretation of every part of the Bible. The Bible is the given "authority" which the would-be interpreter must respect. The Bible as a literary document occupies an important place in the history of mankind. The questions and the thought of many generations have been dominated and fashioned by the Bible and for this reason it deserves respect. As men try to understand the Bible as an influential factor in history and culture, they expose themselves to its influence. But we have to ask whether it is not perhaps misleading to speak of this influence as "authority".

2. When the Church seeks to give an account of itself it has to refer to the Bible. The "authority" of the Bible may be seen as consisting in its character as an indispensable source of knowledge for the Church. Historically the Christian Church grew out of the witness of the apostles and the first Chris-

tian congregations. In all periods, the Church has allowed its teaching to be defined by this Tradition. The Bible is unique as the book in which the witness on which the Church is founded is preserved and accessible in its most trustworthy form. For this reason, the Church has acknowledged this collection of writings as an historical document with which it knows itself to be inescapably related.

3. When we speak of the "authority" of the Bible in the strict sense, we mean that it makes the Word of God audible and is therefore able to lead men to faith. We are not thinking of its authority as a literary document nor of its literary value, nor even of its authority as the oldest documentation of the apostolic message, but of the fact that men are arrested by the message of the Bible, the fact that they hear God speaking to them from the Bible. Ultimately, of course, this authority is the authority of God himself and not that of the Bible as a book. Authority in this sense can only be claimed for the Bible because by its witness it makes possible the knowledge of God and of his authority. Therefore it only has derived authority. Nevertheless, anyone who has once encountered the living God in Christ in the Bible will again and again return to this source.

But is the term "authority" an appropriate one to apply to the Bible at all? Certain groups expressed doubts on this score. The term "authority" is open to many misunderstandings today. It is all too easily associated with authorities demanding blind obedience and therefore suppressing freedom rather than creating it. Authority and status quo are mentioned in the same breath, so that to apply the term authority to the Bible may obscure rather than illuminate the nature and influence of the scriptures. It is, of course, possible to distinguish between "authoritative" and "authoritarian" and to interpret the authority of the Bible in the former sense. But this is a fine distinction and difficult to sustain in ordinary usage. But even more important is a further reservation; certain groups asked whether the Bible can ever be experienced as authority in the sense of a mastering power compelling assent and in this way leading to freedom. Certainly God himself is experienced in this way but can the same be said of the Bible as a "derived authority"? Is it not more appropriate to speak of the "role", the "influence", or the "function" of Scripture (British group)? Reservations about the term "authority" and all its western misinterpretations were expressed from the Orthodox side especially. [4]

While giving due weight to these reservations, most groups retained the term "authority". In their view, the problems arising today could best be

---

[4] *The Ecumenical Review*, Vol. XXI, No. 2, April 1969, pp. 106 ff.

clarified if we started from this concept. But they all stressed that authority must be understood as a "relational concept", not as aggressive power but as a testimony which is to be accepted in freedom, not as overwhelming force but as a gateway to freedom. Authority is therefore a present reality only when men experience it as authority; at the same time, it transcends human experience. Special and explicit emphasis must be placed on this supra-individual character of authority (see Section IV). We cannot restrict the term "the authority of the Bible" simply to the last of the three levels of meaning. We must equally do justice to the understanding of the authority of the Bible in the sense of the "document of the faith of the Church" (see the next section). The various dimensions of the authority of the Bible are not to be divorced from one another.

III. Revelation and the diversity of interpretations

1. The Bible speaks of certain events in history in which God's revealing, judging and saving work has been achieved. Here, however, a difficulty appears which left its mark in the reports of all the groups. If our faith rests on historical events in which God was revealed, then a great deal seems to depend on whether the Bible transmits to us a reliable witness of these historical events. But biblical scholarship has shown us above all that the events which the Bible claims to be decisively important have already in every case been subject to interpretation. Altogether apart from the question of the credibility of such reported events in modern eyes, to get behind the interpretation to the event itself as such proves to be a hazardous and often an impossible business. Every reconstruction of "what really happened" is never anything other than a more or less reasonable hypothesis. This applies as much to biblical research as to the field of secular history. The events reported are therefore never the "bare facts", but are always accessible to us only in the clothing of their interpretation by the biblical authors.

2. This might easily suggest that the authority of the Bible really rests not on the events which it reports but on the interpretation of these events by the biblical writers. Would the authority of the Bible be seriously impaired if the events which it proclaims to be decisively important proved never to have happened at all? The various groups were agreed that there is an indissoluble connection between event and interpretation which is not to be broken on either side. On the one hand, it has to be maintained that there are no uninterpreted events in the Bible. Indeed we must go further and say that the events as such have no revelatory significance at all but are, so to speak, dumb and in need of interpretation if God's voice is to be heard in them. In a sense, therefore, the interpretation is the event. On the other hand, the

historical character of the revelation is of central importance. The relevance of the interpretations rests ultimately on the events to which they refer and by which they are determined. Some were of the opinion that revelation was not bound to what actually happened in history but could even have taken place in the telling of the story (a minority in the British group). But the great majority held that the historicity of the event is of decisive importance.

3. What has so far been said applies equally to the Old and the New Testaments. We look first at the New Testament. Its centre is the "event of Christ". But this one central event has several historical aspects, such as the appearance and ministry of Jesus, his words and teaching, his cross and resurrection. The whole of the New Testament is related to this central sequence of events in Christ. Many passages, however, give direct testimony concerning it, whereas other passages are less directly related to it. To the second group of passages belong, for example, those in which the New Testament writers reflect in various ways upon the redemptive significance of the cross and resurrection, or again, the paranetic passages. The question of historicity arises directly in many of the miracle stories and it also affects central reports such as that of the virgin birth, the empty tomb or the ascension. It is not our concern here to assert or deny historicity. For even apart from the findings of biblical scholarship, we are dealing here with reports which can clarify and interpret the central content of the Gospel, namely, God's action in Jesus Christ.

4. If therefore, in accordance with all we have said so far, it is not the event alone but only the event in association with its appropriate interpretation which reveals God, then the temporal proximity and firsthand character of the Bible cannot be decisive for its authority. It is in principle possible for a later interpretation to be closer in substance to the Gospel. None of the groups was able, of course, to accept an exclusive choice between temporal and substantial proximity. The Dutch-German group in particular raised this question in detail but arrived at no agreed finding. Many held that the eyewitness character of the Bible was of the greatest importance for its authority. It makes clear the indissoluble unity between event and interpretation. Others, while allowing that the New Testament witnesses enjoyed a *de facto* priority by virtue of their temporal proximity, nevertheless maintained that this temporal proximity did not necessarily mean a priority in substance. All agreed that certain New Testament interpretations could be more apt than certain others. The authority of the Bible is based at one and the same time on the temporal and substantial proximity. But if this twofold proximity is claimed for the New Testament witness, one is almost inevitably led to assume something in the nature of inspiration for the text of the New Testament.

5. The New Testament contains various interpretations. All the groups faced this fact. In the interpretations which they worked on, they did not come up against any contradictions which could not somehow be reconciled. This fact may of course have been in part the result of the choice of themes and does not therefore permit any general conclusion. The groups all started out from the assumption that every interpretation was tied to a particular historically conditioned situation and must be understood in terms of that situation. If the interpretations are viewed in this way, they can all be understood as consistent with each other in their different lines of vision to the extent that they all point beyond themselves to the God who revealed himself in Christ; they then show how this truth has been experienced as authority in different situations. But can every interpretation claim to be a legitimate exegesis of a central event? The group which dealt with the virgin birth explicitly raised this question. Did this interpretation have binding authority? Ultimately their answer was yes. For in the group's opinion the meagre testimony to this affirmation (of the virgin birth) was no decisive argument against this legitimacy. Nor was it able to accept the argument that this interpretation weakened the humanity of Christ. But what was not contested was that a critical distinction between various interpretations is in principle possible. The criterion is to what extent an interpretation interprets a central saving event attested in the scriptures and is rooted in that saving event.

6. The Bible presents us with a great variety of material. Different interpretations keyed to different situations stand side by side. How does the voice of God become audible for our present time in this material? Is a centre discernible on the basis of which the whole of the material can become intelligible and fall into place? This is possible to some extent. Clearly the various interpretations do not all enjoy the same weight. The New Testament itself presses certain distinctions upon us. The message of the resurrection is undoubtedly of greater importance than that of the virgin birth. Nevertheless, all the groups were extremely cautious in their conclusions. Though readily accepting that certain interpretations are only of secondary importance, they were against excluding any material at all from the scriptures. That a certain passage failed to speak authoritatively to us and that we could not conceive its ever doing so was no basis for any final judgment about its value. The reason why it fails to speak to our situation may be simply that it is so essentially part of a different situation. But in a new and altered situation it could certainly once more speak to our condition. While, therefore, a discriminating judgment is not only permissible but actually mandatory, yet the body of the scriptures is not necessarily touched by this.

7. Several groups expressly rejected any talk of a "canon within the canon" or of a "material centre" (Sachmitte) either in the New Testament or in the Bible as a whole. True as it is that the interpretations contained in the Bible are not all on the same level, terms like these suggest the possibility of establishing permanent distinctions. It is too easy to interpret terms like "canon within the canon" and "material centre" in a static sense. We cannot, therefore, attribute permanent authority to an inner circle of biblical writings or biblical statements and interpret the rest in terms of this inner circle. But the biblical statements do have certain internal connections and many of these connections are directly related to central saving facts whereas others are derived from these primary statements, as conclusions from them or as fuller explanations of them. Different sets of statements, different writings and groups of writings each have different centres. The Dutch-German group gave special attention to this internal connection of biblical statements. To denote these decisive centres it coined the term *Beziehungsmitte* (relational centre). The love of God or the resurrection of Christ were regarded as relational centres from which the statements about eternal life follow logically. This group spoke of Jesus the Christ, the Kingdom of God, the death and resurrection of Jesus Christ, as relational centres for the entire New Testament, but regarded none of these formulas as exclusive.

8. It is often impossible to adopt the biblical interpretations today without qualification. This does not mean that they are without meaning. The truth is rather that the present generation enters into the process of interpretation in which the witnesses of that past time were also engaged. On the basis of the interpretations they have bequeathed to us we must try to catch a glimpse of the facts which they were interpreting and to do in our situation what they did in theirs. We must act in spiritual agreement with them. As their interpretation was related to God's revelatory action, so our interpretation must be oriented analogously.

9. If the process of contemporary interpretation is seen as the prolongation of the interpretative process which is recognizable in the Bible, then considerable importance must be attached to the situation at any given time in our interpretation of the scriptures. Just as the biblical writers responded to a particular situation, so contemporary interpretation is also determined by our own situation. The questions which are put to the text play a large part in the interpretation. Of course the text has its own weight. It poses its own questions and certain questions which spring from our own situation will find no echo in the Bible. The scope is limited in principle by the reality attested in it. But the situation with its given elements and open problems determines the

perspective within which the biblical witness must be read and interpreted. The reports of the groups make it quite clear that such situation-conditioned hermeneutic perspectives are inescapable. They should not be branded as bias but understood rather as a method of relating to contemporary situations. The American group, for example, decided on the basis of its situation that its hermeneutic perspective was God the Liberator and that it was from this standpoint that the biblical witness had to be read and interpreted. The report on "The Significance of the Hermeneutical Problem for the Ecumenical Movement" had already pointed out this interplay between questions posed by the text and questions put to the text. [5] The Bible can only demonstrate its authority when this interplay is accepted.

10. What is the significance of the canon? It is hardly possible to overestimate its practical significance. The books which have been collected together to form the Bible have become a literary unity which has exercised a profound influence throughout the course of history. The fact that certain writings were included and others excluded has had a decisive influence on the history of the Church. The canon has assembled a variety of witnesses and it is precisely this variety which has determined the history of exegesis. One group, for example, pointed out that the christological debate of the first centuries would have taken a different course ham this standpoint that the biblical witness had to be read and interpreted. The report on "The Significance of the Hermeneutical Problem for the Ecumenical Movement" had already pointed out this interplay between questions posed by the text and questiwhich we ourselves must also enter today in our own way. The dividing line between canonical and non-canonical writings is not a hard and fast one. It is much more a matter of a fluid boundary. As we have already said, even the witnesses included in the canon do not have the same significance. But even though canonicity permits no ultimate judgment about the authority of a writing, nevertheless the drawing of a boundary-line is by no means unimportant. The fact that the Church has acknowledged these writings as the authorized material concerning God's action in Christ, makes the canon of Scripture the testimony which is prescribed for us. It only remains to add that the extra-canonical writings, and particularly the inter-testamental literature, are extremely important for the study of the presuppositions and conditions of the biblical period.

11. Are the considerations mentioned so far also valid for the Old Testament? Most of the groups did not deal at length with this question, especially

---

[5] See *New Directions in Faith and Order*, Bristol 1967. Geneva: WCC, 1968, p.37.

where the selected themes did not compel them to do so. There are different central events in the Old Testament, such as the Exodus, the events at Sinai, the occupation of Canaan, the Davidic monarchy, the return from Exile, all of which are viewed as revealing God's activity and are related in different ways to the divine covenant with Israel for the sake of mankind as a whole. What was said above about the unity of event and interpretation applies also to the Old Testament, and we are confronted in the Old Testament with a plurality of interpretations which do not all have the same weight. But whereas the New Testament is related to one central historical event, the person and life of Jesus Christ, the Old Testament covers a history of many centuries. In the Old Testament, moreover, we find a much greater variety of types of testimony and, to a much greater degree than the New Testament, the Old Testament contains material whose connection with historical events is not apparent to us (the Wisdom literature in particular).

A considerable difference in the assessment of the Old Testament emerges in the group reports. The difference was most clearly formulated by the Dutch-German group: "Some of us hold that, as far as its relational centre is concerned, the Old Testament has an authority equal to that of the New Testament; they therefore speak of two foci of authority which interpret and supplement one another. Others hold that the Old Testament receives its authority for us only through the relational centre of the New Testament; therefore the reciprocal interpretation of the Old Testament and the New Testament is accessible only by way of the New Testament witness." Clearly our reading of the Old Testament will differ in accordance with whichever of these views is adopted. This is the reason for important differences in interpretation.

IV. Holy Spirit, Church and inspiration

Ultimately, the authority of the Bible only becomes evident as the Bible proves itself to be authoritative. Its authority cannot be derived from any external criteria. Certainly the Bible has authority as a literary document which deserves to be read. It is, moreover, of inescapable significance as the authorized testimony prescribed to the Church. But when we speak of the authority of the Bible we do not mean authority merely in this sense. What we mean is rather that through the Bible God proves himself to be the Lord and the Redeemer.

Various considerations have been suggested to try to show the inherent authority of the Bible.

1. The Bible contains a message which is non-derivative and archetypal (*unableitbar*). It is unique in character and has therefore to be accepted. One group, for example, pointed out that the understanding of God in the Old Testament is distinctive and cannot possibly be derived from the oriental religions. Jahweh stands over against all idols and this opposition is a characteristic of the whole Bible. It is precisely in this respect that it proves its authority (Roman Catholic group in Germany).

2. In the history of the Church the Bible has again and again proved to be the source of faith. For this reason it is entitled to insist today that we submit ourselves to its affirmations.

3. In the traditional view, dominant in many churches, the Bible is regarded as an inspired book and its authority is seen as resting on this fact of inspiration. This doctrine of inspiration can take different forms in matters of detail but in any case the Bible is distinguished fundamentally from other books, since in it God has used human words and formulations to reveal himself.

But ultimately none of these considerations provides an adequate basis for the authority of the Bible. The first remains too general and formal. The other two really offer no argument; they either contain a mere assertion or a dogma whose validity is presupposed. The group reports, on the contrary, agree that the content of the Bible must prove itself authoritative and they abandon any attempt to provide an external basis for the authority of the Bible. Indeed they even point out that the authority of the Bible would be diminished if it required legitimation from other sources. It must be capable of proving itself.

But the very fact that it is the impact of its message which demonstrates the authority of the Bible led several groups back once more — much to their surprise — to the question of the inspiration of Scripture. If God's claim is experienced in the compelling way it undoubtedly is in the Bible, does this not mean that behind the Bible is the activity of God himself, i.e. of his Spirit? Is not the witness of the Bible in a special way God's own witness to us? If we speak here of inspiration, it is important to observe the fundamental difference between this use and the traditional doctrine of inspiration. What in the latter is a dogmatic assumption is here the outcome of the experience in which the message of the Bible proves itself authoritative. The assertion that this biblical testimony is inspired remains an utterance of faith. To assume inspiration in advance would lead to a legalistic view of Scripture.

Adoption of the notion of inspiration raises a number of further questions which the groups referred to but did not answer. If the assertion that the Bible is inspired is a conclusion drawn from actual encounter with God through the Bible, the question arises as to why this should only be true of the Bible. Why should not Basil, Augustine, Thomas, Luther or some modern author be inspired too? Surely it was their work of interpretation that led to the Bible's speaking once again with fresh authority. Indeed, why should we not also speak of inspiration in the case of today's preaching which can also lead to an encounter with God and thus prove itself inspired in the same way as happens with the Bible? Obviously a clearer explanation is required as to whether and in what sense God has bound himself through the Spirit to the Bible in its entirety.

The question about the authority of the Bible is inseparable from the interpretative process in the Church. To speak of inspiration, therefore, means reopening the question of the work of the Spirit in the community of the Church. Whenever contemporary interpretation leads men to know the Bible as the work of the Spirit, we have to remember the long line of inspired witnesses which has influenced this interpretation. The first witnesses were called and inspired by the Spirit, but their testimony once it has been given its final form does not become independent of that same Spirit. To be handed on it has to be read in the Spirit. Just as the Spirit once called his witnesses, so today will He also awaken faith, obedience and witness as he opens up to us these indispensable witnesses. The Spirit works in the Church. How is his work in the historical community of the Church related to his work in the individual Christian? Do we not have to affirm that it is only within the community of the Church that Scripture can be read and really heard as God's Word created by the Spirit?

V. The use of the Bible

The complexity of the question of the authority of the Bible became clear to us in the course of our enquiry. This complexity is due to the special character of the biblical material as well as to the variety and variability of the situations in which Christians and churches find themselves in the modern world. Nevertheless, we were able to clarify the concept of authority as applied to the Bible (Section II), to point out the various historical and contemporary aspects of the problem (Section III) and finally, to indicate certain conclusions concerning, in particular, the relationship between pneumatology and ecclesiology.

On the basis of these provisional findings, is it possible to say anything about the question of the right use of the Bible, which we referred to at the very beginning of the report? In what follows our main concern will be to consider the ecumenical implications.

1. We are not to regard the Bible primarily as a standard to which we must conform in all the questions arising in our life. The Bible is witness to the God who gives us freedom in Christ. The calling of the Church is to live in communion with Christ. Therefore we are not to turn this Scripture witness to this God into a law. The Bible's contents need constantly to be unfolded afresh. Its inner unity must become clear. But it is not to be turned into a norm for every problem and every situation. To do so would be to press it too far. This applies not only to fundamentalism but also to the attempt to formulate the biblical view of every problem which happens to come under discussion. The Bible is not a norm imposed on us from outside. On the contrary it is meant to be read and heard within the witnessing community, in the Church. Interpretation is also partly determined by the elements of any given situation. The varied and often widely divergent interpretations which the Bible contains make it an invitation to us to attest in our own words the message which it contains.

2. At the same time, of course, the Bible must be read with the expectation that it can disclose the truth to us. The indispensable confrontation with contemporary thought and the elements of our present situation must not betray us into surrendering the priority of the Bible for the Church's thought and action. The Bible is not a patrimony from which we are free to select at will, nor is it just one source of inspiration among many. To understand it in such a way would be to misunderstand it. The decisive importance of its message for all times is only rightly acknowledged when its testimony is read in anticipation of its disclosure to us of the ultimate sense of our world and of our own lives.

3. The Bible is a critical book. It is impossible to fit it into the generally prevailing thought of the day. Nor is it identical with the doctrine and thought of the Church. It is a critical court of appeal to which the Church must constantly defer and from whose judgment not even the developments taking place in our world are exempted. It is not surprising, therefore, that the question of the right approach to the Bible and of the precise application of its message should lead to vigorous controversies in the Church. It is obvious that the dividing lines in these controversies no longer coincide with the traditional confessional boundaries. Whenever the Church is asked, from inside or from outside, in whose name and by what authority it speaks and acts, the problem of biblical authority also assumes form.

4. The forms in which the biblical message is expressed are inseparably bound up with the historical situation of the people of Israel and of the primitive Church. The biblical writers sought to speak and act in response to the challenges of their own times. The supreme challenge was the message

itself but besides this there was also the confrontation with contemporary movements, such as syncretism, the emperor cult, gnosticism and so on. The message had to prove itself in the midst of constant controversy. The Bible begins to speak most effectively when it is read in the context of the corresponding controversies of our own times. It has, therefore, to be exposed to the challenge of the situation existing at any given time. This also means that the Bible is not a religious book in the usual sense, meant only for use in the liturgy. It has, on the contrary, to be brought into a two-way relationship with the questions of the time.

5. If the contemporary situation is incorporated in this way into the interpretative process, it is clear that agreed methods of exegesis in no sense inevitably produce agreed findings. The universally acknowledged authority of the Bible is no guarantee of the Church's unity. But the contemporary interpretative process is in fact simply the continuation of the interpretative process which begins in the Bible itself. Only by constantly renewed interpretation does the one message remain a living Spirit and not a dead letter. This sheds new light on the problem of the right relationship between unity and diversity, and between norm and change. How can the Bible prove its authority in face of the changes of our time which lead to so radical a criticism of traditional claims to authority? How can we interpret the message of the Bible in such a way that, at one and the same time, its authority is respected and it sets us free to understand the demands and opportunities of our present time?

And, above all, how is the Bible to be so interpreted that there may be a genuine unity in Christ? Perhaps our present experience in dealing with the Bible may also lead us to a new understanding of unity. Certainly the ecumenical movement in which Christians of different traditions face together the challenges of their times provides the setting where these questions can be raised afresh. And as we in this movement learn to use the Bible aright, the Bible will also demonstrate its power afresh.

5. The Significance of the Old Testament in its Relation to the New

The committee which evaluated the report on the "Authority of the Bible" at the Faith and Order Commission meeting in Louvain (1971) recommended that "the relationship of Old and New Testaments and particularly the contemporary significance of the Old Testament should be given careful study". Acting upon this recommendation, the Faith and Order Secretariat requested a group of theologians from several churches in The Netherlands to draw up a report which could serve as the basis for further discussion. The group complied with the request and worked out the paper "The Relation Between Old Testament and New Testament" (WCC archives FO/73:20). It was discussed at the Faith and Order Working Committee meeting in Zagorsk (1973) and the following year in an open hearing at the meeting of the full Commission in Accra. There it was recommended to continue the study by soliciting reactions to the paper by individual scholars and groups from as many different sides as possible.

A considerable number of answers were received. They were summarized in a synopsis by Dr Ellen Flesseman-van Leer (WCC archives, Loccum consultation, 1977). With the Dutch paper and the synopsis before them, a small group drawn from the membership of the Faith and Order Standing Commission met in Loccum (West Germany) in July 1977 and drew up the report printed here (WCC archives FO/78:2) which was approved by the Standing Commission meeting in Bangalore (1978). It appears here for the first time in print.

*　　*

*

> *The churches are divided in the way in which they use and understand the Bible. At the same time, however, they proceed in the hope that a common use and understanding will bring them together. The authority and interpretation of the Bible are inescapable questions for them, on which they have already worked for a long time. What applies to the Bible in general, applies in particular to the Old Testament.*

The starting point

1. We want to affirm at the outset that we are speaking from within the Church. In the Church as the universal fellowship of believers in Jesus Christ the Bible has a decisive authority. This authority is not merely an outward authority, but it becomes a living and present reality, when it is also experienced and received as such. Thus we understand the authority of the Bible as a "relational concept" whereby the Bible places the recipient under its inherent authority and the recipient hears and accepts this authority.[1] This authority applies both to the Old and the New Testament as the common tradition of the Church maintains. Taking our stand in this tradition, *we want in this report to develop particularly the place and contemporary significance of the Old Testament in its relation to the New Testament.*

2. This study has emerged out of work which dealt with the hermeneutical principles for the interpretation of the Bible and with biblical authority.[2] That work left the inter-relatedness of the Testaments and the value and specific interpretation of the Old Testament still unresolved. These are exactly the questions on which there are still considerable differences of opinion among the various churches. Moreover, since we started our study it has

---

[1] This thought is developed at greater length in the study report "The Authority of the Bible", presented to the Faith and Order Commission at Louvain 1971 (*Faith and Order, Louvain 1971.* Geneva: WCC, 1971, pp. 9-23). There it is stated: "Authority must be understood as a 'relational concept', not as aggressive power but as a testimony which is to be accepted in freedom, not as overwhelming force but as a gateway to freedom. Authority is therefore a present reality only when men experience it as authority; at the same time, *it transcends human experience. Special and explicit emphasis must be placed on this supra-individual character of authority*" (14). We want to draw particular attention to the words which we have underlined, because they are often left out when this passage is quoted. The result is then that "relational concept" is misunderstood as if it were human experience which attributes authority to the Bible.

[2] Attention should be drawn to the following reports: "Guiding Principles for the Interpretation of the Bible", accepted by the ecumenical study conference at Wadham College, Oxford 1949 (*Biblical Authority For Today.* London: SCM Press, 1951, pp. 240-243); "The Significance of the Hermeneutical Problem for the Ecumenical Movement" (*New Directions in Faith and Order, Bristol 1967.* WCC: Geneva, 1968, pp. 32-41, presented to the Faith and Order Commission at Bristol 1967; and the Louvain report, mentioned in the former note.

become increasingly clear that its subject has implications for many other issues which have arisen, in particular for the dialogue with people of other faiths and ideologies. In this report we have not been able to elaborate those issues in detail. What we try to do here mainly is to formulate those insights which have a direct bearing on our central theme and which may help the churches to a deeper common understanding of the Bible.

PART I: THE PROBLEM

The Old Testament canon
   3. When we think about the Old Testament the question immediately arises: which Old Testament are we dealing with? Many churches consider the Greek version, the Septuagint, to be their canonical Old Testament Scripture; many other churches, especially of the Reformation tradition, accept the Hebrew text of the Masora as normative. No translation can avoid an interpretative element and the Septuagint is no exception. It does not only render the Hebrew text which lies behind it, but also interprets it at the same time. In the Greek version words and concepts have often lost their Hebrew flavour and received a new connotation, and sometimes entire sentences and passages are changed in a hellenistic direction.[3] Thus, whenever the Septuagint is used, it fosters a more positive evaluation of hellenizing and spiritualizing tendencies than when the Masora is used.[4] In addition, the Septuagint canon comprises a larger body of Jewish wisdom and apocalyptic literature than the Hebrew canon. The consequence is that when the former is normative, creation, natural revelation and moral rules will receive greater emphasis, and Jesus will be seen more in an apocalyptic light. In the Masora, on the other hand, the Torah and the pre-exilic and exilic prophets with their messages of judgment and hope play a more central role and history is a more important factor. This means that the Old Testament is understood different-

---

[3] The difference between the Masora and the Septuagint can not only be explained through differences created by the translation process. The Septuagint has also preserved alternative Hebrew reading different from, but as old or even older than, the text of the Masora.

[4] The Bristol report stressed the importance of studying the Bible in the languages in which it was written, basically Hebrew and Greek, because it regarded "the original text and language as a meeting point for all scholars" (35). Though this observation is valid as far as scholarship is concerned, the report failed to notice that for many churches the original Hebrew version is not the canonical, authoritative Old Testament.

ly, depending on which version of it is being used. This, in its turn, affects the understanding of the New Testament. We can conclude from the above that the fact that the churches have different normative versions of the Old Testament constitutes a divisive factor, which needs to be overcome for the sake of their future unity. [5]

The use of the Old Testament in the churches

4. The Old Testament functions in the churches in different ways. There is in the first place the *liturgical* use. In churches which have a fixed lectionary of Scripture readings in their worship, Old Testament lessons are sometimes included. This is to be welcomed, because it helps to preserve some knowledge of the Old Testament. However, there is the danger that texts, read out of context and heard by people with little background knowledge, become formalized and what they are saying is no longer heard or understood. When psalms are used in the liturgical life of the Church they are often used in what we may perhaps call a "participatory way". The worshippers find in them expressions of their own joy or sorrow, or they join in them as hymns of praise and thanksgiving, or as prayers for deliverance from distress. In such cases all historical distance falls away. In a feeling of immediacy and contemporaneity Israel is identified with the Church and its king with Jesus Christ. In the same participatory way individual Christians may use the Old Testament in their meditative or devotional life.

5. Further, the Old Testament functions in the teaching and preaching ministries of the churches. There is a *narrative* use, employed particularly in teaching children, there is a *doctrinal* use, often used in teaching adults, and a *homiletic* use found in expository preaching. This latter use is found particularly in churches of the Reformed tradition where sermons are often based on texts taken from the Old Testament.

6. In recent times most uses of the Bible have been affected to some degree or other by modern biblical scholarship. Against the background of the Enlightenment, the literary critical and historical critical methods have been developed. This has led to the temporal remoteness of the Bible in

---

[5] The Louvain report, in speaking about the significance of the canon, noted that "it is hardly possible to overestimate its practical significance. ... The canon has assembled a variety of witnesses and it is precisely this variety which has determined the history of exegesis." On the other hand, the report played down the *theological* significance of the canon by stating that "the dividing line between canonical and non-canonical writings is not a hard and fast one. It is much more a matter of a fluid boundary" (18). True as these remarks may be, the report omits mentioning the fact that still today different canons can be a determining factor for the churches in their different overall understanding of the Bible. Therefore, the limits of the canon have greater theological implication than the Louvain report implied.

general, and more particularly of the Old Testament, being keenly felt. On the one hand, these methods have had a unifying effect on the interpretation of the Bible; but, on the other hand, they have also proved a new divisive factor, for there is difference of opinion, both within and between churches, on how far such critical methods are valid. Moreover, biblical criticism can lead to an intellectualization in which the texts remain a thing of the past and their immediate impact on the present believer is blunted or never taken into account.

7. But not all churches have felt equally that there is this historical gulf between the Bible and the Christian today, which has to be overcome consciously. The African independent churches are a case in point. In the context of our present study these churches are of particular interest because of the great importance they attach to the Old Testament which they read with an attitude of almost unquestioning contemporaneity. Many African Christians identify themselves so closely with the Old Testament that they consider it to be really their own book. The symbolism in the Old Testament speaks to them immediately in their own cultural background and they have no difficulty in recognizing themselves in many cultural, social, political and cultic elements of the Old Testament. If anything, they have easier access to the Old than the New Testament. In view of the above it is not surprising that sermon texts are often taken from the Old Testament and that the African preacher has no difficulty in bridging the historical gap between the Old Testament and present-day believers. There is a timeless continuity between the two.[6]

8. At the present time the role which the Old Testament plays has grown, due largely to the greater attention which churches and Christians pay to political and social questions and to the way in which black Christians in North America, Christian revolutionary groups in Latin America and Christian Marxists there and in Europe experience and express their Christian faith. These groups have in common that they put a particular Old Testament

---

[6] Beside this attitude of unreflective immediacy towards the Bible there are also thought-out hermeneutical approaches which presuppose a view of contemporaneity. The Bristol report, one sidedly, paid attention only to the literary-and historical-critical methods. Though we agree with the report when it states that these methods are today "necessary ones" (33), because they are the best tools we have to safeguard the "over-againstness" of the biblical texts, we have become more conscious of the fact that critical scholarship is not the only possible hermeneutical approach. A few years later, the Louvain report called attention to the method of structuralism as a sophisticated version of a synchronized view of the Bible and the present-day reader (11f). Since then still other hermeneutical approaches have come to the fore which stress more the immediacy of the biblical text than its remoteness, such as the literary approach with its close reading method and the political approach with its maxim that only to someone who is actually involved in the political struggle the Bible discloses its meaning. It should however be noted that these other approaches do not necessarily reject the critical method.

motif, such as the Exodus motif with its emphasis on liberation from slavery or the concern of the eighth century prophets for the poor, at the centre of their thinking, and their theological interpretation of the Gospel is determined by such specific Old Testament motifs.

Historical continuity and its evaluation

9. Undoubtedly there exists a historical continuity between the Old Testament and the New Testament. Jesus, of whom the New Testament bears witness, was a Jew, and He lived his life among the Jewish people, of whose history the Old Testament speaks. Also, the Bible of the early Church was formed from the holy books of the Jews. But the Church with its New Testament is not the only continuation of the Old Testament. Rabbinic Judaism and the history of the Jewish people since the time of Jesus are also historical continuations of the Old Testament and the history of Old Testament Israel. Islam, too, to a lesser degree has roots in the Old Testament. In this paper we do not go into the question of how we theologically evaluate the significance of the two other religions which have grown out of the Old Testament, nor do we ask what theological role the Old Testament plays in them, but rather we concentrate on the Old Testament in the Church.

10. All Christians agree that, because of the historical continuity, the Old Testament is needed in order to understand the New Testament. It is necessary to know the history, faith and spirituality of the people of Israel in the Old Testament if one wants to understand the Jewish background and milieu of Jesus and the early Church. In passing, it should be added that this claim is equally valid for the knowledge of the inter-testamentary literature.

11. But while all accept this value of the historical continuity between the Testaments they are not of one mind when it comes to its evaluation. We have singled out three different types of evaluations, although we are aware of the fact that there are more and that combinations between them are possible.

i) Some attribute no decisive theological significance to the historical continuity; for them the importance of the Old Testament lies in the fact that it gives background knowledge for understanding the New Testament, as expressed in the preceding paragraph.

ii) Others see in the New Testament a re-reading and a reinterpretation of basic Old Testament affirmations[7] in the light of the life, death and resurrec-

---

[7] The notion of re-reading and reinterpretation is taken over from the Louvain report, which talked about "the interpretative process which is recognizable in the Bible" (18, 23). However, there this interpretative process is not considered in its bearing on the relation of Old and New Testament, but rather as pointing to the necessity of interpreting the Bible always anew in response to the challenges and problems of the situation existing at any given time.

tion of Jesus. Therefore, the historical relationship between the Old and the New Testaments has for them also theological significance.

iii) Still others agree with the last mentioned theological position, but emphasize more strongly the theological value of the historical continuity and see more theological implications therein. They maintain that through Christ the Church is engrafted into God's history with the Old Testament people of Israel.

12. These different evaluations, outlined above, are important not only because they have a direct bearing on the value attached to the Old Testament, but also because they determine the view taken about the relationship between the Church and the Jewish people and about the question of what role the Old Testament can play in the meeting of Christians with people of other faiths and ideologies.

The Church and the Jewish people

13. With regard to the relationship between the Church and the Jewish people, those who do not see any theological significance in the relationship between Old and New Testament and thereby implicitly deny any specific theological value to the Old Testament for Christians do not attribute a special place to the Jewish people in God's economy of salvation either before or after Christ. (It should be added that those Christians who interpret the Old Testament only in an allegorical and typological way, and in this way do indeed attribute theological value to it, do not attach any special importance to the Jewish people either.) Those who hold one of the two other positions, that is, who do attach a decisive theological significance to the relationship of the Testaments, believe that in the time before Christ the Jewish people had a special function in God's design for the salvation of the world. Whether after the coming of Christ they still maintain a special place remains a hotly debated issue among Christians. Some years ago, a report, "The Church and the Jewish People", [8] was devoted to this subject; in view of what is said below in this study on the theological significance of the Old Testament, this theme needs to be taken up again and considered further.

---

[8] Presented to the Faith and Order Commission in Bristol 1967 (*New Directions* pp. 69-80). The report stated: "We are convinced that the Jewish people still have a significance of their own for the Church ... it seems to us that by their very existence in spite of all attempts to destroy them, they make it manifest that God has not abandoned them. In this way they are a living and visible sign of God's faithfulness to men, an indication that he also upholds those who do not find it possible to recognize them in his Son" (73). But the report showed too that there remained serious unresolved problems. A more recent report, is the statment "CCJP Contribution to DFI Guidelines" adopted by the Jerusalem Conference of CCJP, 1977. In this report the main controversial issue is whether Jews should be invited to accept Jesus Christ, or whether they "are faithful and obedient to God even though they do not accept Jesus Christ as Lord and Saviour".

The Old Testament and people of other faiths

14. Concerning the meeting of Christians with people of other faiths[9] and ideologies, we have already indicated that the question of what role the Old Testament has to play in such dialogues is answered differently according to the theological value attached to the historical continuity between the Old and the New Testament.

i) The position which denies its specific theological relevance often goes together with, or even stems from, a strong emphasis on the lordship of God over the whole of creation and history. People of other faiths and ideologies are then believed to have each their own place in God's economy of salvation. This means that although initially Christ is known through the witness of the New Testament seen against its Old Testament background, He must essentially be understood within each of these faiths and ideologies in its own terms and thought-structures. Just as originally a Judeo-Christian and later a Hellenistic-Christian Christology was developed, so Hindu-Christian, Buddhist-Christian or Marxist-Christian Christologies must be worked out in our time.

15. (ii) The second of the above-mentioned postions can lead to the conviction that in the re-reading and reinterpretation of the Old Testament by the New, Christians have a theologically significant model for their relationship with people of other faiths. For just as in the New Testament the Old is taken up and at the same time critically reinterpreted in the light of Christ, so Christians living in other cultures and religious traditions must preserve, but reinterpret critically, their cultural and religious heritage. The relation between the Old and the New Testament provides thus a key for interpretation.

16. (iii) Those who adhere to the third position and believe that the Church is engrafted into the Old Testament people of Israel may maintain that God in his freedom has chosen in particular the people of Israel and Jesus Christ as his instruments to make himself known in all places and times. For this group the Old as well as the New Testament is normative; therefore Christians are called to bear witness among people of all other faiths and ideologies to the content of the statements of faith made in both Testaments. Moreover, not only is the relationship between the two Testaments exemplary for the way in which all cultural and religious heritages are to be reinterpreted in the light of Christ, but also the dialectical attitude of the Old Testament towards its surrounding religions, using and reinterpreting those elements of them which could be appropriated and categorically rejecting

---

[9] When we speak in the following about other faiths we do not include Judaism and Islam, because their relation to the Old Testament is of a different kind (see paragraph 7).

those other elements which were incompatible with the faith in the true God, indicates what the attitude of Christians to other religions and ideologies should be.

17. The three theological evaluations of the relationship between the Testaments do not necessarily lead to the convictions which we have described. Much further study of the relevance of the Old Testament to people of other faiths and ideologies is needed before we can reach a common understanding. [10]

PART II: COMMON PERSPECTIVES

One subject and one Scripture

18. In Part I we have described how, although none of them want to ignore it, Christians differ when it comes to assessing the importance of the Old Testament. For some it has an incidental or at least purely historical significance, others attach to it an essential and theological value. Now, in Part II we no longer speak descriptively. We want to affirm our belief that the Old Testament is of decisive and theological importance for Christian faith. Therefore, at the outset, we wish to emphasize the unity of the whole Bible.

19. The Bible is a collection of many varied books which in their two collections are held together by one subject. We meet in them one and the same God in his dealings with his whole creation, with the nations and with individual people. It is he who creates the unity in the diverse testimonies of Old and New Testaments. In the Old Testament we see him dealing particularly with one specific nation and through this nation with all people; in the New Testament we meet him essentially in Jesus Christ, his fullest and decisive revelation, calling his people from among all nations. This God of the Bible shows himself to be that God who wants human beings to be his partners in sustaining the world and in fulfilling the plan he has for it. He is the one who says: "I am your God, you are my people."

20. No single concept can fully express the richness of the relationship which God seeks with his world. One good and biblical way to speak about it is by means of *covenant* terminology. Covenant is one of the most central themes which bind together the two Testaments. First we are told of the covenant God made with the whole of creation through Noah; then comes the

---

[10] In the statement adopted by the Theological Consultation on Dialogue in Community, held at Chiang Mai in 1977 by DFI, one of the questions which was singled out for future study was that of the authority of the Old Testament, as it relates to the dialogue with people of other faiths and ideologies. Therefore we felt compelled to make a first rather tentative attempt to consider that problem as far as it touches on our central theme.

covenant with Abraham, father of all believers; next the covenant made through Moses with the people of Israel and renewed under Joshua and Josiah; with the rise of king David we hear of the covenant with the Davidic house and in the book of Jeremiah we meet the promise of the new covenant to be written on the hearts of men and not on tables of stone. Finally comes the culmination of this theme, the establishment of the new covenant in Jesus Christ.

21. Important as covenant is, there are also other themes which bind the two Testaments together. Another major theme which is common to them both and which expresses an essential element in relation of God and man is that of *hope*. Believers both in the Old Testament and the New Testament look forward to the day when the contradiction between existence as it is experienced and as it is meant to be is done away with. For those who were wandering about, without a dwelling place which they could call their own, there was the hope of land and a large posterity; for those who were living under alien oppression there was the hope of liberation from slavery; for those who were beset by enemies, the hope of victory. Later we are told of hope for universal knowledge of the Lord and of peace within or passing beyond the boundaries of the present world; and still later of hope for life beyond death and of hope that God's will shall fully be done and his glory appear; finally there is found the hope of all hopes that God shall be all in all. This theme of hope is emphasized in the deuterocanonical literature with its apocalyptic expectation. In this respect this literature forms a strong link between the Old and the New Testament.

22. Still another central theme in both Testaments which expresses something of the relationship of God and his creation is that of *wisdom*. It is through wisdom that human beings can participate in God's creative action and it is through wisdom that they are brought to the fear and knowledge of the Lord. God has created the world through wisdom and it is again wisdom that holds creation together and constitutes its inherent order. But there were also the sceptics who saw wisdom no longer as a human possibility but as the possession of God alone. It is this very divine wisdom which appears in Jesus Christ, rejected as folly by the wise and powerful, but accepted by the weak and the sinners. Again the deuterocanonical writings are important here forming a link between the Testaments with their emphasis on wisdom. [11]

---

[11] The Wadham document describes the central concern of the Bible as "God's gracious and redemptive activity for the saving of sinful man that he might create in Jesus Christ a people for himself" (241). The notion of central concern comes close to what the Louvain report called the "material centre" (*Sachmitte*). However, the Louvain report was rather hesitant to speak of one *Sachmitte*, but preferred to speak of various centres, for which it coined the term *Beziehungsmitte* (relational centre). The major themes we mention in our report as constituting the unity of the Testaments can be seen as relational centres for the whole of the Bible.

The unity of the Testaments and the notion of history

23. The question arises whether the theological unity of the Testaments can be described in terms of history. This question can be asked in view of the expressions of faith contained in the Bible, and in view of the divine-human encounter. Regarding the first aspect, we can undoubtedly speak of continuity or development of human faith, though this development should not be understood as an evolution from a lower to a higher form. The history of human faith which can be discerned in the Bible is not an unbroken, upward-going line; there are high points and low points in it and dead-end roads and new beginnings. But we have described the unity of the Testaments not primarily in terms of human faith but in terms of God's relation with his creatures. The issue is then whether one can speak of an ongoing history between God and man. [12] We are not of one mind in this respect.

24. Some of us do believe that the divine-human relationship expresses itself as an ongoing stream in history. There are many blockages in this stream. Again and again it seems to approach its end, but each time it resumes again until it reaches its culmination in Jesus Christ and God becomes fully manifest in him. In his life, death and resurrection a new and unheard of impetus is given to God's history with man.

25. Some others among us believe that such a continuous line is absent and that God's action cannot be historicized in this way. They are inclined to compare the relation between the Old Testament and the proclamation of Christ in the New Testament not with a line but with a circle around its centre. God's manifestations in Israel and in Jesus Christ are not successive events within human history. In Jesus Christ God has fully disclosed himself; his manifestations in Israel are anticipatory disclosures, all equally related to Christ as their centre.

The specificity of the New Testament

26. The specificity of the New Testament, in so far as it surpasses and goes beyond the Old Testament, is primarily Jesus Christ himself. In him appears the one, sent by God, who fully does God's will. In his life, death and resurrection God has completely expressed himself in his love for man in order to make us his true associates.

---

[12] We are aware that we have touched here the problem of the connection between event and interpretation, which is dealt with in the Louvain report (*Louvain 15*). The scheme of event/interpretation has since been repeatedly criticized and clarification has been demanded. We did not go into this problem, which we felt to be a side issue to the topic of this paper.

27. In the *incarnation*, in which the Word itself became flesh, God came to his world and involved himself in it in so intimate a way as is unparalleled in the Old Testament. He made manifest himself and his will and established his bond with man in an unambiguous way which surpassed all He had done before.

28. In his *suffering and death* Jesus Christ is proclaimed as the suffering servant of God, who through his unique sacrificial life and death reconciled the world with God and opened up a new possibility for all human beings to live as forgiven sinners. Thereby the cultic laws and institutions of the Old Testament lost their relevance.

29. In the *resurrection* of Jesus Christ the ultimate destiny of individual human life and of universal history has become manifest. It has become clear that life and history cannot be fulfilled within the limitations of this world, but that the final goal of life is a life beyond death and the final goal of history a total transformation of the world beyond all its existing possibilities. Thereby the Old Testament belief about the finality of death and the conviction that God's dealings with his creatures is limited to life on this side of death is superseded and annulled, and the Old Testament hope of a world of perfect peace and righteousness is transposed, so that its consummation transcends history.

30. As the *Holy Spirit*, the Spirit of the crucified and risen Christ, is poured out upon all flesh, the message of the Old Testament receives a new, universal dimension. For the Spirit, who through baptism incorporates men and women into the Body of Christ, aims at the creation of the Church as a worldwide community of people of all nations in whose midst He brings the Bible alive and fashions it into an instrument for his worldwide activity. Thereby the attention which in the Old Testament is directed mainly to God's work upon a particular nation is extended to the whole world, love and justice among men are no longer restricted within the boundaries of one people, and such things as holy wars and the annihilation of conquered enemies are rejected. This same Spirit is also the power which works for the renewal of men and women in a radical obedience according to the image of Christ. Thus, in the New Testament as compared with the Old, more emphasis is placed on the personal decision of faith, greater value attached to the individual and more attention given to the spiritual and invisible.

31. However, it should be noted that already in the Old Testament an inkling or beginning is found of many of the things in which the New Testament surpasses the Old Testament. We can detect for example the seeds of a belief in immortality and of universality and find places where the individual appears more important than the community.

Various meanings of fulfilment

32. Often the specificity of the New Testament is expressed by the notion of fulfilment. However, this term needs to be carefully used because it is mostly found with the connotation that the Old Testament has become obsolete and is finished. Sometimes fulfilment has indeed the connotation of abrogation, as can be seen in the case of the cultic laws. But the term fulfilment has many more meanings, so that we doubt whether it is very helpful to define the relationship between the two Testaments by this concept. In order to avert wrong implications we have thought it useful to deal with this notion more elaborately. The New Testament and dogmatic theology speak of fulfilment in Christ of the scriptures, the time, the law and the promises.

33. When the New Testament says that in Christ the *scriptures* or certain scriptural sayings have been fulfilled, it means that certain events or elements of proclamation mentioned in the New Testament are not mere accidents but are expressions of the same will of God, which manifested itself already in events or proclamations in the Old Testament. Thus there is a close connection between these New Testament elements and the Old Testament events or proclamations. This connection is established in many different ways and cannot be limited to what is commonly referred to as predictions which have come true.

34. The New Testament phrase that in Christ the time has been fulfilled means in the first place that the moment appointed for him by God has now come. In the coming of Jesus, God himself came to the world; therefore God's dealings with Israel and in Israel with all men have reached their decisive point. Thus, the expression means that in Christ time and history have reached their goal. The question immediately arises about the implication of this statement. For after Christ our human history still continues and its final goal has not yet been achieved. The whole of history is still under an eschatological reservation and nothing is definitely finished. In this respect the witnesses of the New Testament stand beside those of the Old Testament; they too look to the future in which they expect the manifestation of the final victory of God. But in Christ the realization of this future victory has already been inaugurated and the end and goal of history have appeared within history. Thus Christ is both the guarantee that time and history have meaning as well as the norm by which all human history is judged.

35. The thought that Christ has fulfilled the *law* has to be understood in several different ways. In the first place it means that Christ has made transparent the true intention of Old Testament law as a means of God's care for man; thereby its abuse as an instrument of human self-justification is exposed. Further it means that in the light of Christ certain ordinances,

especially those relating to the Old Testament cult and legal system, were seen to be no longer relevant and therefore abrogated. It also means that Christ himself kept the law as the rule of love towards God and towards their fellowmen. It is precisely by being universalized and reinterpreted in this way that in following Christ all sorts of Old Testament ordinances have gained a new relevance. [13]

36. References to Christ's fulfilment of Old Testament *promises* should not just be interpreted in terms of realization but also in terms of confirmation. The promises and expectations of the Old Testament are often fulfilled in such totally unexpected ways that in their fulfilment they appear to have received a radical reinterpretation; often they can only be recognized as being fulfilled in Christ on the basis of this reinterpretation. Thus, every fulfilment proves to contain an element of surprise. The same thing is indeed true inside the Old Testament; here also fulfilments of promises are repeatedly found which come with an unexpected reinterpretation. It becomes clear too that every fulfilment is only a partial one. The promise is greater than the fulfilment; moreover, in its very fulfilment the promise often grows beyond itself and thereby remains valid. Thus the Old Testament expectations of a total renewal of man and of the world are both redeemed in a real but anticipatory way and at the same time confirmed by the coming of Jesus Christ. This confirmation implies that Christ, by fulfilling the Old Testament promises, has opened the road to a still further fulfilment of them. Therefore, it would be incorrect to condense the relation between the Testaments into the model of promise/fulfilment. This becomes still more clear when it is remembered that the Old Testament contains much more than promises. It has its own fulfilments and it speaks no less about God's presence in the past and the present than about his presence in the future.

37. The preceding reflections all go to show that the Old Testament is not finished or antiquated after the fulfilment in Christ, nor that it is enough to consider the Old Testament as just a preparation for Christ. With the continuation of history after Christ the Old Testament is given a new chance. In the light of the Spirit which bears witness to Christ, the Old Testament needs to be continually re-read and reinterpreted.

The specificity of the Old Testament

38. But perhaps even more attention should be given to those things in which the Old Testament surpasses the New Testament, because they are

---

[13] The Wadham document called Jesus Christ both the fulfilment and the end of the Law. It elucidated the meaning of these words no further. We would not like to use the term "end" in this general way, because it seems to preclude the thought of a re-validation and a re-interpretation of the law.

the Old than in the New Testament. It is mainly from the Old Testament that we come to know God as the Creator of all that is, as the Lord of history, as the Judge who upholds the rights of the poor and downtrodden. There too his holiness, majesty and hiddenness are emphasized, his concern with world politics, his exclusive claim upon his creatures and what the Old Testament calls his jealousy. Other specifically Old Testament notions are the creation of man and woman in the image of God, their place in the cosmos as God's caretakers, and the much greater attention given to nature; the warning against the constant temptation to idolatry, the fight against the deification of any part of creation and the danger of a dead, formal religion; moreover the interest in social structures, the insistence on righteousness, the fight against poverty and oppression, the concern with sorrow and the complaint of having been forsaken by God, and the importance of faith in providing wisdom for everday life. All these elements are assumed in the New Testament and most of them are mentioned too. However, they receive there less explicit attention because the New Testament is focused on the appearance of Christ and the radicalization of faith and on the individual conduct of life which comes with it. These specifically Old Testament elements should not be neglected. Otherwise we might come to misconstrue the context within which the appearance of Christ happens, thus running the risk of placing him in a wrong framework — possibly an individualistic, introverted or idealistic one. As a consequence the New Testament would be robbed of its purport. Especially in our time, with its worldwide ethical and structural problems, we need the width and depth of the Old Testament more than ever.

Re-reading the Old Testament

39. When we, who live in the time of the new covenant, meet God in the Old Testament, its words come alive for us in an entirely different situation.[14] Believing that it is and was the same God now and then, the Church, since New Testament times, has been convinced that the Old Testament could speak to her authoritatively in her new and different situation. However, this authority must not be allowed to become arbitrary. That is always the danger when an attitude of contemporaneity of the text with the present-day reader is assumed (see paragraphs 4 and 7), for this attitude disregards what the text in its own historical context intended to convey. But the words and the situations of the Old Testament (and the same goes for the New Testament too) do not permit arbitrary reinterpretation and actualization. To counteract this

---

[14] See for a fuller treatment of the problem of historical remoteness the Louvain report 11f.

danger, a synchronized reading of the text should be accompanied by an approach which uses methods of modern critical scholarship. These methods by themselves are certainly no guarantee either that the Old Testament is really understood (see paragraph 6). The appropriation of the Old Testament by the Church takes place in the tension between careful listening to what was said in the past and its being made relevant for today, and it is the crucified and risen Christ who illumines and reinterprets the Old Testament through the Spirit.

40. This process of actualization of the Old Testament, begun already within the Old Testament itself, is found in the New Testament too. The authors of the New Testament are constantly appealing to Old Testament texts. It is true that they interpreted these texts in ways with which we may often have difficulty. The New Testament writers took over the various exegetical methods which were current in their time, such as the method used by the Jewish rabbis (midrash) or in the Qumran community (midrash pèsher) or by hellenized Jews like Philo (allegorization). These methods are by and large no longer ours; rather, as they used the methods of their time, we should use the best exegetical methods of our time. Consequently, our interpretation of Old Testament texts will often differ from the one found in the New Testament or, to say the least, the meaning we perceive in Old Testament texts will not be exhausted by their New Testament interpretation. But that is not to say that we are allowed to disregard the use of the Old Testament by New Testament writers. On the contrary, we should try to understand carefully the witness to Christ which they gave by their, to us often no longer convincing, interpretation of Old Testament texts.

The kerygmatic use of the New Testament and the Old Testament

41. It seems appropriate to conclude our observations on the significance and understanding of the Old Testament in its relation to the New Testament with a paragraph on the kerygmatic use of the Bible in the preaching of the Church, because many of the things we have been saying come to a head there.

42. In preaching from the New Testament the Old Testament should be taken into consideration. (i) Knowledge of the Old Testament world of thought is indispensable for the understanding of many New Testament words, concepts and thoughts. New Testament ideas are often derived from Old Testament ones; their full connotation will only be understood when they are, as it were, translated into their Old Testament counterparts. (ii) Many thoughts of the New Testament, particularly those of a more individual and spiritual nature, have to be counterbalanced by the more cor-

porate and this-worldly thinking of the Old Testament, otherwise the biblical message will be distorted. (iii) Jesus Christ is God's deed par excellence. This will only become manifest when God's preceding deeds, to which the Old Testament bears witness, are taken into account also. Moreover, the Old Testament is the foil against which the new things which Jesus Christ has brought are to be set in order to appear in their newness. Thus, in every sermon from the New Testament the Old Testament must provide the background — whether explicitly or not.

43. In preaching from the Old Testament, the name of Jesus Christ will often present itself to us so naturally and emphatically that we will mention him explicitly. We cannot lay down any one pattern in which this should be done, for the connections which we can make between the Old Testament and Christ are varied and manifold. Sometimes the Old Testament may point to Christ in a typological or preparatory manner; or again it may speak of a promise which has been fulfilled in him; sometimes it may bring Christ to mind because of a particular contrast. Also freer, more playful connections can be made, as when allegory or free associations are employed. None of these forms can be rejected out of hand, but neither can exclusive validity be claimed for any one of them. But because the Old Testament is more than mere preparation for Christ and has still a validity of its own, it also can be preached in the Church without any specific reference being made to Jesus Christ or the New Testament. For the Old Testament has its own kerygmatic worth. Such proclamation from the Old Testament must never be in contradiction to the main line of the New Testament. For the Spirit which makes the words of the Old Testament, as well as those of the New Testament, come alive for today is the Spirit of Christ. Therefore, just as the Old Testament forms the background for the New Testament, Jesus Christ is the horizon for the Old Testament.

PART III: ECUMENICAL RELEVANCE AND RECOMMENDATIONS

Ecumenical relevance

44. The primary importance of this study for the ecumenical movement is so self-evident that it hardly needs spelling out. The WCC states in its Basis that its member churches confess Jesus Christ according to the Scriptures. These words "according to the Scriptures" should be given their full weight, as they were explicitly added to the Basis at the Third Assembly in New Delhi, 1961. The Old Testament is an integral part of the scriptures. Therefore, any clarification of its importance and understanding is to be

welcomed — the more so because considerable differences exist among the churches on that account.

45. In order to give a credible witness to the world, the churches have to be one. Difference of opinion as to the importance and the understanding of the Old Testament has been a divisive factor. This report might help to overcome these differences and thereby pave the way to attain unity in witness. This unity in witness is also of importance in the dialogue of Christians with people of other faiths and ideologies. The differences of opinion about the role of the Old Testament in this dialogue were mentioned above (see paragraphs 14-17). This uncertainty impairs both the dialogue and the unity of the churches. In those respects too this study might be of help.

46. Social and political problems have become hotly debated issues among Christians. It is particularly the Old Testament to which appeal is made for decisions in those matters. This appeal to the Old Testament has become a new cause of strife and disunity which cuts right across the lines of the churches. A better understanding of the authority and the specificity of the Old Testament will be of help in overcoming these new divisions.

47. One of the main hindrances to the unity of the churches as well as within many churches is the polarization between those who are said to absolutize the "vertical" over against the "horizontal" dimensions of Christian faith and vice versa. When the Old Testament and the New Testament are seen in their interaction — and it is clear from this report that it is an interaction full of tension, correction and enrichment — it becomes an indication that both dimensions should not be played off against one another and it provides a directive for the way in which conflicts and tensions in the churches are to be dealt with. The Old Testament can save the New Testament from a one-sided "vertical" and other-worldly misunderstanding and the New Testament can save the Old Testament from a too "horizontal" and merely this-worldly misunderstanding.

Recommendations

48. In the course of our study some points have come to the fore to which further thought should be given. Therefore, we recommend as follows:

(i) It is important that the churches should have a common version of the Old Testament canon. It is a matter of course that the original text was in Hebrew; moreover, scholarship has shown that the inter-testamentary literature is of great importance as a link between the Old and the New Testament. We suggest, therefore, that the churches use as normative the Masora or whatever Hebrew text modern scholarship, with its method of textual criticism, considers to be the best and most authentic one together with the deuterocanonical writings. This is precisely what is done in the modern ecumenical translation of the Old Testament, the French TOB.

49. (ii) The churches might ask themselves whether the Old Testament has an adequate place in their worship and their teaching. Specifically, they might reconsider in this respect their lectionaries, their sermons and their catechetical material.

Those churches which use the Old Testament mainly liturgically might pay specific attention in their teaching ministry to what the Old Testament intended to say in its own situation and context, using the insights of modern criticism. Those churches which use the Old Testament mainly in their teaching ministry might be encouraged to learn from the liturgical use which other churches make of the Old Testament.

As a matter of course all churches are selective in their use of the Bible and particularly of the Old Testament. But care should be taken that this selective use is not unnecessarily one-sided and that the main sections of the Old Testament all receive appropriate attention.

50. (iii) Above we have made a few remarks on the Old Testament in its relation to people of other faiths and ideologies. That issue has to be worked out in much greater detail. In particular, we would suggest two themes: (a) The different attitudes which we have described in paragraphs 14-16 should be rethought. (b) The role of the Old Testament as such in the dialogue with people of other faiths and ideologies should be considered. It might be useful that a collection of articles, each of them dealing with the contribution of the Old Testament in the respective dialogues, be published.

51. (iv) In paragraph 13 we have mentioned the report of Bristol on "The Church and the Jewish People". The problem with which that report dealt is still a burning issue and a challenge to the unity of the churches, as a more recent consultation of CCJP in Jerusalem 1977 has shown (see note 13). We believe that an understanding of the significance of the Old Testament has an immediate bearing on it. Therefore, we would hope that the entire issue might be taken up again.

Selected Bibliography

Note: Only those publications are listed here, in chronological order, which in the context of the World Council of Churches deal with biblical interpretation and authority, and relate explicitly to the reports printed in this booklet. Titles mentioned in the introductions to the reports are not repeated here.

De Dietrich, Suzanne: *Le renouveau biblique, hier et aujourd' hui. I: Qu'est-ce que la Bible? II: Comment lire la Bible.* Neuchâtel, 1969. The original book was published in 1945. This is a revised edition, bringing it up to date.

De Dietrich, Suzanne: "The Bible, a Force of Unity." *The Ecumenical Review*, Vol. I, No. 4, 1949, pp. 410-416.

The Bible and Church's Message to the World: an Ecumenical Inquiry. Geneva: Study Department, WCC, 1949.

Schweitzer, Wolfgang: "The Bible and the Church's Message to the World." *The Ecumenical Review*, Vol. II, No. 4, 1950, pp. 123-132.

Biblical Authority for Today, ed. A. Richardson and W. Schweitzer. London: SCM Press, 1951. Most of the writers of the articles collected here had taken part in one or more of the study conferences on "The Biblical Authority for the Churches' Social and Political Message Today" organized by the Study Department of the World Council of Churches in the years 1946-1949.

Chirgwin, A.M.: "Have the Bible and its Circulation Any Significance for the Ecumenical Movement?" *The Ecumenical Review*, Vol.VI, No. 3, 1954, pp. 295-299.

Visser 't Hooft, W.A.: "The Bible and the Ecumenical Movement." *Bulletin of the United Bible Societies*, 1963, 4th quarter.

Schrift und Tradition, ed. K.E. Skydsgaard and L. Vischer. Zürich: EVZ Verlag, 1963. This book contains the articles of the members of the European section of the Commission on Tradition and Traditions. An English translation of the articles by Ebeling, Flesseman-van Leer, Greenslade and Bonis is available in the Montreal files under TCTT II/a,b,c,d.

Käsemann, Ernst: "Unity and Diversity in New Testament Ecclesiology." *Novum Testamentum,* 6, 1963, pp. 290-297. The original German version: "Einheit und Vielfalt in der neutestamentlichen Lehre von der Kirche", can be found in *Exegetische Versuche und Besinnungen,* II. Göttingen: Vanden Hoeck & Ruprecht, 1964, pp. 262-267. Address given at the Fourth World Conference on Faith and Order, Montreal, 1963.

Brown, Raymond E., SS: "Einheit und Verschiedenheit in der neutestamentlichen Ekklesiologie." *Okumenische Rundschau,* Vol. 13, 1964, pp. 63-73. The original English version of this conference address can be found in the WCC archive files under Montreal/10.

Nelson, Robert A.: "Scripture, Tradition and Traditions." *The Ecumenical Review,* Vol. XVI, No. 2, 1964, pp. 158-163.

Cahill, P.J.: "Scripture, Tradition and Unity." *Catholic Biblical Quarterly,* Vol. 27, 1965, pp. 315-335.

Gaybra, Brian: *The Tradition: an Ecumenical Breakthrough? A Study of a Faith and Order Study.* Rome: Herder, 1971 (dissertation at the Pontificia Universitas Urbaniana, Rome, 1967).

Voss, Gerhard: "Die ökumenische Bedeutung der biblischen Hermeneutik." *Una Sancta,* Vol. 23, No. 1/2, 1968, pp. 35-49.

Flesseman-van Leer, Ellen: "Introduction à une étude sur l'autorité de l'Ecriture au Conseil Oecuménique des Eglises." *Foi et vie: Cahiers bibliques,* Vol. 6, 1968, pp. 72-78.

Dinkler, Erich: "Bemerkungen zu zwei ökumenischen Arbeitsthemen. Das Problem der biblischen Hermeneutik — Die Kirche und das jüdische Volk." *Okumenische Rundschau,* Vol. 17, No. 3, 1968, pp. 273-287.

Dinkler, Erich: "Die ökumenische Bewegung und die Hermeneutik." *Theologische Literaturzeitung,* Vol. 94, 1969, pp. 481-490.

Rowe, Richard C.: *Bible Study in the World Council of Churches.* Research pamphlet No. 16. Geneva: WCC, 1969.

Sallie, James Samuel: *Scripture and Tradition in Protestant Ecumenism Since the World Conference on Faith and Order, Lund 1952,* 1969 (dissertation). Microfilm available in the WCC library, Geneva.

Marlé, René, SJ: "Le problème de l'herméneutique à Foi et Constitution." *Recherches de Science religieuse,* Vol. 58, 1970, pp. 101-112.

Weber, Hans-Ruedi: "The Bible: Contested and Contesting." *Study Encounter,* Vol. VI, No. 4, 1970, pp. 173-178.

Weber, Hans-Ruedi: "The Bible in Today's Ecumenical Movement." *The Ecumenical Review,* Vol. XXIII, No. 4, 1971, pp. 335-346.

Pesch, Rudolf; Starobinski, Jean; Argenti, Cyrille; de Mello, Manoel: "The Healing of a Demoniac. Different Approaches to Mark 5:1-20." *The Ecumenical Review,* Vol. XXIII, No. 4, 1971, pp. 347-418.

Dupuy, B.-D., OP: "La conférence de Louvain." *Istina,* Vol. 16, 1971, pp. 271-273.

Flesseman-van Leer, Ellen: "Biblical Interpretation in the World Council of Churches." *Study Encounter,* Vol. 8, No. 2, 1972.

Weber, Hans-Ruedi: "The Bible: Central Guide for the Ecumenical Movement." *Journal of Theology for Southern Africa,* No. 1, 1972, pp. 23-36.

Flesseman-van Leer, Ellen: "Dear Christopher." In *What About the New Testament? Essays in Honour of Christopher Evans,* ed. Morna Hooker and Colin Hickling. London: SCM Press, 1975, pp. 234-242.

Beckwith, Roger: "The Use of the Bible in the World Council of Churches." *Churchman,* Vol. 89, No. 3, 1975, pp. 213-224.

Schrotenboer, Paul G.: "The Bible in the World Council of Churches." *Calvin Theological Journal,* Vol. 12, No. 2, 1977, pp. 144-163.

Runia, K: *De Wereldraad in discussie,* met reacties van E. Flesseman-van Leer, H. Berkhof, A.H. van den Heuvel. Kampen: Kok, 1978, pp. 18-28, 125-129.

Printed in Switzerland